C0-AYG-678

PROGRESS AND ARCHÆOLOGY

PROGRESS
AND ARCHÆOLOGY

By

V. GORDON CHILDE, D.Litt., D.Sc.

Department of Prehistoric Archæology, University of
Edinburgh

GREENWOOD PRESS, PUBLISHERS
WESTPORT, CONNECTICUT

0491400   70857

Originally published in 1944
by Watts & Co., London

First Greenwood Reprinting 1971

Library of Congress Catalogue Card Number 70-114499

SBN 8371-4779-4

Printed in the United States of America

CONTENTS

0491400

70857

70827

CHAPTER I

THE PROGRESS OF ARCHÆOLOGY

" DIGGING up the past " has now come to be generally
recognized as not only an exciting pastime, but also
a serious science, so that many people want to know
what it is all about. The glamour of excavation
cannot, indeed, be recaptured in a few brief pages.
A bare enumeration of spectacular finds from the
disinterment of Pompeii in 1748 to the discovery of
the ship-burial of an Anglo-Saxon king in 1939 and of
the glittering tomb of Pharaoh Sheshonk in 1940
would be more tedious than instructive. Even less
palatable would be a compressed outline of the speculative and controversial reconstructions of historical
events—folk-migrations, religious reformations, and
social cataclysms—extracted by prehistorians and
historians from such finds. Are there no more comprehensive results, general conclusions, and principles
to be drawn from the vast array of isolated facts
excavators and collectors have so industriously and
patiently amassed?

In certain branches of the study, at least, archæology does disclose trends and developments all tending
in one definite direction, and consequently cumulative
and progressive in effect. It is the sole aim of this
book to set forth concisely the most clearly and confidently recognizable of these progressive tendencies
as they have operated during at least 50,000 years.
Domains in which either the author for his part
(e.g., in costume and graphic art) or any archæologist as such (e.g., in music and spoken language)
can recognize no such predominantly one-way
trends will be simply ignored. But first what is
archæology?

The objects of archæology are any alterations in
the earth's crust and in natural objects upon it in so
far as they have survived at all. Archæology, in

fact, furnishes a sort of history of human activity, provided always that the actions have produced concrete results and left recognizable material traces. It turns into history whenever it remembers that the objects it studies embody the thoughts and intentions of human beings and societies. But in its own transformation, archæology has revolutionized history. It has enlarged the spatial horizon of history in much the same degree as the telescope enlarged astronomy's vision of space. It has extended history's view backward in time a hundredfold, just as the microscope revealed to biology beneath the surface of gross bodies the lives of infinitesimal cells. Finally, it has altered the content of historical study in much the same sort of way as radioactivity affected chemistry. For one thing, archæology is largely concerned with practical everyday things, contrivances and inventions like houses, drains, axes, and internal-combustion engines that in themselves have affected the lives of far more people, and that far more profoundly, than any battle or conspiracy, but that formerly seemed beneath the dignity of scholarly history.

A century and a half ago human history, apart from its mythological prelude, covered about 3,000 years. For at least half that time its horizon was strictly limited by the Alps, the Judæan hills, and the Sahara. It was based exclusively on written texts, and for most people consisted of lists of kings and battles, political revolutions and theological controversies. Nevertheless even in the sixteenth century artists and architects had been seeking inspiration in the extant monuments of Greco-Roman civilization. After 1738 these were explored more systematically to assist scholars in the interpretation of the Classical texts that still formed the basis of a gentleman's education. In the ruins of Pompeii the ashes erupted from Vesuvius in A.D.70 had preserved a vivid picture of the life of a provincial Roman town, but even in distant Britain the spade could lay bare the roads along which the conquering legions marched and the camps from which they dominated the island's " natives."

From the close of the century historical archæologists set out to explore in the same spirit what had been left by earlier peoples whose names at least were familiar from Classical and Hebrew authors—the Egyptians (from 1797), the Assyrians (from 1843), and the Babylonians. As a result the decipherment of Egyptian hieroglyphics (1819) and the Babylonian cuneiform writing (1837) unlocked another 2,000 years of written history that has, however, always been studied in constant relation to the more substantial remains left by its authors.

In the meantime men of leisure and country doctors had begun to examine the monuments built by their own illiterate ancestors and the rude utensils these had left behind, their prime aim being of course to supplement the curt descriptions of Celts and Germans given by Roman historians. Gentlemen gathered large collections of native arms and vases to set beside curios from the South Seas, Grecian urns, and miscellaneous junk. The necessity of arranging such collections methodically forced antiquaries to devise a system of classification, and that was the first and indispensable step to making archæology a science.

Obviously, once the use of antiques had been determined (and that was settled by common sense, an appeal to ancient writers, or, most profitably since the sixteenth century, by comparison with the implements still being made and used by savages in America and the South Seas), the basis for their classification must be chronological. But in so far as they were " prehistoric," made and used by illiterates, they bore no date of manufacture. Now the Greeks and Romans had known that men used tools and weapons of bronze before iron, and of stone before bronze. By 1836 J. C. Thomsen had arranged the prehistoric collection in the National Museum of Northern Antiquities at Copenhagen in accordance with the

principal industrial material, dividing the relics between Stone, Bronze, and Iron Ages.   The framework
he applied has worked so well that it still forms a
basis for the systematic arrangement of remains from
the illiterate past in a chronological order.   And in
1854 Thomsen's Stone Age came alive in Switzerland;
the lowering of lake-waters by an exceptional drought
exposed the remains of villages wherein had been
preserved by the waters, like the habitations of
Pompeii by volcanic ash, not mere fragments of
tools such as had hitherto been collected, but stone
axes in their perishable wooden handles, baskets,
textiles, the very bread eaten by Stone Age men.

But by then an infinitely earlier phase of the Stone
Age reaching back into the geological past was coming
into view.   In 1797 John Frere recognized stone
implements apparently associated with bones of extinct animals at Hoxne.   Next century Buckland in
Wales, Lartet and others on the Continent, began
finding remains of human handiwork and even human
skeletons in caves with bones of mammoths and
reindeer, though Buckland at least refused to believe
his own eyes.   And near Abbeville, Boucher de
Perthes was recovering humanly shaped flints in the
still older gravels of the Somme.   French experts
rejected the human workmanship of these finds or
their antiquity.   But in 1859 John Evans and Prest-
wich visited Abbeville, and their conversion secured
the final acceptance of Boucher de Perthe's contentions.
The pleistocene age of our species was established
and human history released from the narrow confines
of Bishop Usher's chronology that is still printed in
the margin of the Authorized Version of the Bible.

In the same year Darwin published *The Origin of
Species*.   The mass of evidence there marshalled by
Darwin, and his plausible account of the process,
secured the acceptance of the theory of *Evolution*.
Thereby Man became a part of Nature and Human
History a continuation of Natural History.   At the
same time Nature acquired a history as much as Man.

The static hierarchy of immutable and fore-ordained species and genera accepted by earlier naturalists dissolved into historical events, results of observable processes of the same kind as those studied by the historian of human societies. In 1859 prehistoric archæology, and so history as informed by archæology, may be deemed to have become a science. On the foundations then laid archæology has grown with constantly accelerated velocity both in content and in clarity of interpretation. Only one general result of that growth can be even mentioned in this introduction.

Archaeologists have reached some measure of agreement on a tentative and provisional chronology to establish not only the order in which events happen at any given place, but also a more comprehensive framework within which events at different places can be compared. The sequence of events at any given place is termed their *relative chronology* and is settled in the last resort by written evidence or, in default of such, by what is termed stratigraphy. When the sequences are the same at several sites they give a series of consecutive periods applying to a whole province and described by conventional names. For instance terms like Tudor and Jacobean are used to designate archæological periods in English history. Such names tell us nothing about the duration of the periods nor yet about their relation to archæological events in other provinces such as France, or even Scotland, but indicate only position in a series. Prehistoric periods are similarly designated, e.g., the Hallstatt and La Tène periods within the Iron Age this side of the Alps.

Of course Thomsen's three " Ages " are just periods of this relative kind and would be better designated *Stages*. Stone, Bronze, and Iron everywhere follow one another in that order. But in absolute time the Stone Age ended before 3500 B.C. in Mesopotamia, about 1600 B.C. in Denmark, and A.D. 1800 in New Zealand! Moreover the Stone Age is enormously longer than either of the others. By

1859 it was recognized that it must be subdivided. One division will contain those remains associated with extinct animals or otherwise assigned to the geological past—the pleistocene; to the other will be confined relics and constructions of the geologically *Recent* era or holocene. To these major divisions Lubbock in 1863 gave the names—*palæolithic* (Old Stone) and *neolithic* (New Stone) respectively. Since 1900 a *mesolithic* (Middle Stone) Age has been inserted after the Palæolithic to contain archæological events that are later than the pleistocene but older than the emergence of a Neolithic as defined on p. 12.

Absolute chronology, the reference of these " periods " or " stages " to some universal time-scale, is much harder to fix, and is often still very speculative. Of course where written records are available it is comparatively easy to discover that for instance the Tudor period in England covers the years A.D. 1500 to 1600. Thereby the archæological events thus designated find a place in a series of solar years reckoned from an arbitrary starting-point—the Christian era—and applicable to the whole globe. So we know at once what is the counterpart of Tudor architecture in another region, say China—but not in Australia, where no written record goes back so far. In practice written sources do not take us back very far. In England they take us back to A.D. 40, in France to 60 B.C., in Italy a little beyond 500 B.C., in Greece before 700, but nowhere in our continent before 1000. In China written records are available as early as 1400 B.C., in Asia Minor to 1800, only in Egypt and Mesopotamia to 3000 B.C. Before that everything is absolutely prehistoric.

As long as written records were being kept any-where there is always a chance of linking up events in illiterate regions with historical events, owing to the remarkably widespread interchange of materials and goods described in Chapter V. The later dates here given for events this side of the Alps or in Iran are based on such supposed contacts, but they are admittedly only approximate.   Indeed, even in fully historical epochs archæological events can seldom be dated to within less than ten years, and here we can be content to reckon in centuries or half-centuries.

For still earlier phases the best chronometer and standard is provided by geological or climatic changes affecting considerable areas of the earth's surface. The remains of plants preserved in the peat mosses of the British Isles, Northern Europe, the Alps and the Urals allow botanists to deduce, still in the Recent epoch of geologists, a series of consecutive climatic phases to which the names *Pre-Boreal, Boreal, Atlantic, Sub-Boreal* and *Sub-Atlantic* have been respectively applied.   These phases form a convenient general framework within which to view events over quite a large area, but not strictly an absolute chronology since they are still unrecognizable in the Mediterranean basin, Africa and southern Asia.

Still earlier, in the geological pleistocene, prolonged periods of intense cold produced great ice-sheets to cover most of Britain, North Germany and Scandinavia and tremendous glaciers in the Alps, the Pyrenees, the Atlas and the Himalayas.   Many geologists believe there were four such *Ice Ages* or *Glacials*, separated by more genial intervals or *interglacials*. Others admit only three, others on the contrary nine. Apart from this uncertainty it is difficult to recognize the counterparts of ice ages in warm regions like the Mediterranean, Africa and Further Asia.   There is a good deal of evidence for two (or even three) periods of heavy rainfall or *pluvials* in regions now oppressed with constant drought like North Africa, Rhodesia, Syria and Iran, but how ice ages and pluvials should be correlated is still a matter of dispute.   Could these doubts be resolved the succession of ice ages would provide a real *absolute* chronometer, though the units of time it marks must be reckoned not in years or even centuries, but in millennia and tens of millennia. For convenience in exposition I have assumed four pleistocene ice ages and two pluvials corresponding respectively to the first and the last *pairs* of ice ages.

Attempts to express in years the duration of the pleistocene and succeeding phases are still more provisional. Zeuner and Paterson have each tried to correlate ice ages and interglacials with Milanković's curve showing in millennia the varying amounts of heat from the sun reaching the earth's surface. I have adopted Zeuner's figures to give the reader some notion of the magnitudes that *may* be involved. For the same reason I have adopted de Geer's figures for the duration of the earlier post-pleistocene phases of climate in the North. The important and agreed points for the reader to remember are: the pleistocene epoch is at least 10 times as long as the recent; the recent is at least 3 times as long as that covered by the oldest historical records of Egypt and Mesopotamia; since the Old Stone Age (palæolithic) falls entirely within the pleistocene, but may not altogether coincide with it, it is at least 5 times as long as all other archæological periods together; written history covers about one-hundredth part of human history and that only in a tiny corner of our large planet. The accompanying tables will set forth these results as they will be used throughout this book.

The terms *savagery*, *barbarism* and *civilization* sometimes used in the succeeding chapters technically denote successive stages in social and economic development as defined particularly by the ethnographer Morgan and the economist Engels, but do not exactly coincide with the archæological " ages " just defined and have even less chronological implications. A *savage* society here means one that depends for its livelihood exclusively on hunting, fishing and collecting, whereas all *barbarians* augment their food-supply by cultivating edible plants, breeding animals for food or combining both activities. The term *civilized* is reserved, in conformity with the word's derivation, for people who dwell in cities; and a *city* must possess not only a certain size, but accommodate a substantial minority at least of persons who derive their livelihood not directly from hunting, fishing or farming, but from secondary industry, trade and other professions. In archæology it is convenient to take the discovery of inscribed objects, and so the use of

TABLE I.—The earlier archæological stages with their probable geological equivalents and estimated duration in years, after Zeuner.

1 Years.	2 Geological Period.	3 Archaeological Culture.	4 Archaeological Stage.
0 —	RECENT	See Table II	Mesolithic
50,000 —	ICE AGE (Würm)	Magdalenian — — — — — Gravettian	Upper Palæolithic
100,000 —		Moustierian	Middle Palæolithic
150,000 —	Interglacial 3	Levalloisean Clactonian Chelleo-Acheulian	
200,000 —	ICE AGE (Riss)		- - - - - - - - -
250,000 —			
300,000 —	Interglacial 2		Lower Palæolithic
400,000 —			
	ICE AGE (Mindel)		? Eolithic
500,000 —	Interglacial 1		
	ICE AGE (Gunz)		
600,000 —	PLIOCENE		

All later archæological periods occupy such relatively short times that they cannot be shown separately on this scale. Table II continues the above on a scale one hundred times as great.

Table II.—Later archæological and historical periods.

Years.	Hither Asia.	Egypt.	Greece.	North-western Europe.	Climatic Phase.
A.D. 1000	Islamic	Islamic	Byzantine	Dark Ages	
500–					
0–	Parthian	Roman	Roman	Roman	
	Seleucid	Ptolemaic	Hellenistic	La Tène (Iron Age)	Sub-Atlantic
B.C. 500–	Persian	Persian	Classical	Hallstatt (Iron Age)	
	Neo-Babylonian		Archaic Dark Age		
1000–	Assyrian			Late (Bronze Age)	
				Middle	
	Hittite	New Kingdom	Mycenaean		
1500–	Kassite			Early (Bronze Age)	Sub-Boreal
	Babylonian	Middle Kingdom	Middle		
2000–	Dark Age	Dark Age			
	Age of Ur III				
	Akkadian		Early Minoan and Helladic		
2500–		Old Kingdom		Neolithic	
	Early Dynastic	Proto-dynastic			Atlantic
3000–	Jemdet Nasr				
	Uruk	Predynastic	Neolithic		
	al'Ubaid				
4000–	Halafian	Merimdian		Mesolithic	
	? Neolithic Sialk I		?		
5000–					
6000–	? Natufian				Boreal
7000–					

writing, or literacy, as the criterion of civilization. Barbarian villages or townships may be comparable in area to cities; they may have housed an appreciable number, albeit always a small minority, of craftsmen like smiths, carpenters and even potters; imported materials and manufactures may be collected from their ruins, but such will seldom have been indispensable to the average townsman save for arms. To decide when the quantitative expansion of population and multiplication of craftsmen and merchants has produced a qualitatively new entity, the city, writing is a good test. (In *Man Makes Himself* I have explained how writing was necessitated by economic developments and is generally connected with the change from a kinship to a territorial basis of social organization.)

CHAPTER II

THE FOOD QUEST

MAN must eat to live at all; food is perhaps the one absolute and overriding need for man. In early and primitive societies the quest for food was and is the most absorbing preoccupation for all members of the group. The enlargement of the food-supply was therefore presumably the indispensable condition for human progress. In deciding what societies of the past ate, and how they procured it, archæologists rely on the actual remains of food, but also on the location of settlements and most of all on the tools of production, including under the latter term not only movable things like fishhooks and ploughs (*relics*), but also the remains of ancient fields, irrigation canals and such like *monuments*. Combining these sources of information we can recognize two outstandingly contrasted stages in the food-quest, food-gathering and food-producing. In any given region such correspond at first to the archæological " ages " termed respectively palæolithic (or Old Stone) and neolithic (or New Stone). All palæolithic—and so-called mesolithic—societies, like *savage* tribes in Australia, in African and Malayan jungles and in the Arctic to-day, seem to have lived parasitically on nature by collecting, catching or hunting wild fruits, roots, grubs, game or fish. Neolithic societies on the contrary co-operated with nature to increase their food supply by cultivating plants or by breeding edible animals, or by combining both activities as mixed farmers. On the basis of the neolithic economy further advances could be made in what archæologists term the Bronze and Iron Ages (Stages) in that farmers produced more than was needed for domestic consumption to support new classes, not engaged in growing or catching their own food, but in secondary industry, trade, administration or the worship of gods.

12

In the archæological record these successive advances are reflected in the emergence of appropriate tools. A closer study of these will reveal in each of the main divisions a progressive series of sub-stages. In the first division, the Old Stone Age, that is nearly a hundred times as long as all the rest, we can conveniently distinguish the eolithic, lower, middle and upper palæolithic and add, if we like, a mesolithic at the end. Not even the lowest known of modern savages, the Tasmanians, used such imperfect tools made by such clumsy methods as those of the eolithic and lower and middle palæolithic ages; no living race is so apelike as Pekin man or even middle palæolithic Neandertal man. Upper palæolithic men, however, were as well equipped as modern savages and physically differed little from existing races.

Pekin men, who lived somewhere between 500,000 and 250,000 years ago, apparently already caught and ate wild animals, mostly now extinct; their bones, split as if to extract the marrow, and even scorched by fire as if the meat had been cooked, are found in the cave at Chou-kou-tien near Pekin, where these ape-men lived. But among the stone tools found in the cave, as among other eoliths, there is none that can be regarded as a specialized weapon of the chase; indeed, they are so shapeless that it is impossible to say exactly what they were used for.

Lower palæolithic tools have been more skilfully and more intelligently made and include standardized forms, but none of these strikes us as an efficient weapon. In so far as men of this stage ate meat, they must have relied upon drives, assisted probably by natural missiles and sharpened sticks. Under such conditions the chase cannot have been very productive, and an enormous area would have been required to support a small human group.

First about 150,000 to 90,000 years ago, when the last severe ice age was approaching in Europe, are specialized weapons recognizable. They are pointed, triangular flakes suitable for attaching to wooden

shafts as the points of thrusting-spears, but too
clumsy for missile weapons. With such a spear the
hunter could pierce the hide of a rhinoceros. With
their aid the Neandertal men of the European Moustierian were able to secure regular supplies of mammoth meat during the first part of the last ice age.
But in Moustierian caves are found also rounded
stones that have been interpreted—on rather inade-
quate grounds—as belonging to some composite
missile like the South American bola.

The invention of really effective and penetrating
missile weapons, or rather the development of the
technical skill and the equipment requisite for making
such, may be taken as distinctive of the upper palæolithic phase. It must have revolutionized hunting.
By this time a number of distinct social groups can be
recognized in the archæological record. The Aurignacians, who lived in caves in the hills of Palestine,
the Crimea, the Balkans, and Central and Western
Europe some 80,000 to 60,000 years ago, made ingenious dart-heads of bone or ivory. For the fabrication of these, specialized secondary tools of flint were
of course needed. With their aid herds of wild
horse, bison, and other gregarious beasts were pursued
with marked success.

About the same time in South Russia, and rather
later in Western Europe, the Gravettians armed their
missiles with tanged flint points that would pierce
even the mammoth's tough hide. Knowing how to
construct adequate shelters to withstand arctic blasts,
they frequented the tundras and steppes where these
great pachyderms browsed, and from cleverly located
camps took toll of the great herds in their seasonal
migrations. Enormous bone-heaps, buried in the
löss that was then accumulating on the steppes, mark
the sites of their encampment and the success of their
food-quest.

In North Africa a group known as the Aterians
converted the middle palæolithic triangular flake into
a light dart-head by applying the new technique of

pressure-flaking, thinning down the flake by the removal of scales from both faces. Alternatively they reduced the same sort of flake to a small tanged and barbed point exactly like an arrow-head. So presumably they possessed a bow. Now the bow is one of mankind's first mechanical inventions (see *Man Makes Himself*, p. 67). It opened up immense new possibilities to the huntsman, especially in the pursuit of small agile game like the gazelles and antelopes of the North African steppes. Other African societies, the Capsians in North, the Kenya-Aurignacians in East, Africa probably used the bow too, but they presumably armed their arrows with the puzzling little *microliths*—minute but very carefully shaped crescents and triangles of flint—that are so common on their camp sites. The invention soon spread to Spain; arrow-heads turn up while the Gravettian culture was still flourishing there. North of the Alps and Pyrenees the bow is first attested in the mesolithic stage. Before that, however, at least the Magdalenians, the descendants of the Gravettians in Western Europe, and perhaps the Gravettians themselves, had learned to extend the range of their missiles and to improve their aim by using the spear-thrower, a device still employed by the Australian aborigines and the Esquimaux.

The Aurignacians of the Crimea and France already caught fish; the bones of large river-fish and simple clumsy bone-gorges have been unearthed in their caves. Their successors in France, the Magdalenians, improved the gorges and began making also fish-spears or harpoons of reindeer antler. The successive layers in the caves reveal the development of such spears from rudimentary forms with a single row of small barbs to quite efficient implements with big barbs on both edges. Fishing on well-stocked rivers would guarantee a regular supply of food and encourage tribes to abandon nomadic life and settle down more permanently beside the favoured reaches.

By the close of the European ice age the gathering

economy had attained a pitch of efficiency scarcely surpassed by even the most advanced savages—the Red Indians of British Columbia or the Esquimaux. With the products of the chase and fishing, the Magdalenians could enjoy a relatively settled life, and even secure a surplus to support specialists devoted to the cultivation of magical art. But this comfort and prosperity was due to favourable circumstances alone. With the final disappearance of the glaciers the open steppes became covered with forests, the mammoths died out, the herds of bison and reindeer departed, and salmon sought new spawning-grounds. The large communities that had been supported by collective hunting and fishing in France and Russia had to break up and learn new techniques.

In the mesolithic period that followed, simple gathering—the collection of snails, shell-fish, and nuts —came into fresh prominence, judging by the high proportion of such in the food-refuse of the period, both in Europe and also in North Africa. But the great size of the shell-heaps would seem indicative of a relatively sedentary life. In Europe the new forest game—red and roe deer, wild pig, otters, birds —must be pursued with bow and arrows. The arrows were generally tipped and barbed, as earlier in Africa, with the tiny geometric flints termed microliths that are among the most easily recognizable relics of the mesolithic stage. At the same time man found a partner and helper in the chase— the dog—whose aid would be most useful in the pursuit of just that game the post-glacial landscape provided. So from the Crimea to Portugal the bones of wolf-like dogs are found first in mesolithic settlements.

Subsequent developments of the gathering economy down to modern times follow divergent lines in different environments. For instance, on the forested plains of Northern Europe the hunters and fishers seem to have been still largely nomadic in Pre-Boreal times, to have shifted annually from summer to

winter camps during the Boreal phase, but to have
settled down in permanent encampments beside good
fishing-grounds or oyster-beds in the Atlantic, at the
same time improving their technique, notably by the
invention of proper barbed fish-hooks of bone and
of nets with floats and sinkers (both in Boreal times),
and naturally of the instruments necessary for their
manufacture. But by this time the new productive
economy was already supplementing food-gathering
among more progressive or more favourably situated societies.

The first still ambiguous hints of the new economy
come from Palestine, where some botanists believe
the wild ancestors of wheat and barley grew spontaneously. A tribe conveniently termed Natufians,
inhabiting caves in Mount Carmel and elsewhere,
lived, indeed, by collecting, hunting, and fishing with
the usual mesolithic tackle of flint microliths and
bone "harpoons." But they made also saw-like
flints mounted in bone handles, the edges of which
show a peculiar lustre that experiment proves can be
produced only by cutting straw.

Such flints are therefore *sickle* teeth. Whether
they were used for cutting cultivated grains or just
wild grasses has not yet been determined. Now to-
day the number of barbarians who cultivate plants
but breed no animals for food far exceeds those who
practise mixed farming. But apart from the Natufians
it is mixed farming that is first represented in the
archæological record.

Well before 4000 B.C. the new economy is clearly
illustrated in Egypt and Iran by communities settled
in the Fayum depression, at Merimde on the western
edge of the Nile Delta, and at Sialk, an oasis on the
western borders of the desert basin of Central Iran.
All these communities still relied mainly on hunting,
fowling, and fishing (with bows and arrows, harpoons,
and hook-and-line in Egypt, with slings and clubs in
Iran). But all cultivated plants and bred sheep and
cattle, and in Egypt pigs. For from all sites survive

the bones of stock, the lustred flint blades of sickles—
at Sialk mounted in bone handles identical with the
Natufian—and the primitive handmills or saddle-
querns on which the grains were ground to flour. In
Egypt the actual grains—emmer wheat and barley—
have been preserved, and also the silos in which the
crop was stored. For a decisive consequence of
agriculture is that the cultivators not only can, but
must, store up grain to last till the next harvest;
thrift is obligatory.

In Iran, and probably also in Egypt, the crops were
watered by irrigation. At the same time the muddy
water restored to the soil most of the salts extracted
from it by the crop. Hence the same plot could be
cultivated year after year without losing its fertility,
so that the farmers could live on at the same site.
At Sialk the ruins of successive mud huts, repeatedly
rebuilt, had formed mounds or *tells*, totalling 90 ft.
in height, before a new economy ushered in the
historical period about 3000 B.C. In Egypt Merimde
and the Fayum settlements were abandoned, but a
series of great cemeteries along the Nile itself take up
the tale till the villages grew into cities, again about
3000 B.C. In both areas the development thus disclosed runs in the same general direction: the mixed
economy of gathering supplemented by farming
gradually gives place to one based on farming, with
hunting as a subsidiary occupation or relegated to
distinct social groups; new food-plants are grown in
the gardens, fresh species added to the farmyard.
And throughout Hither Asia the neolithic economy
looks much the same, as the excavators' spades lay
bare its deeply buried remains.

In the temperate zone of Europe, where neolithic
settlements have been known much longer, they bear
a very different aspect. In the oldest villages farming
is already much more important than hunting or
collecting. For instance, in the very oldest pile-
villages built on the shores of Swiss lakes, 70 per cent.
of the animal bones recovered are those of domestic

stock. Among the Danubians of the Central European löss lands hunting- and fishing-tackle is almost entirely missing, all animals' bones are rare, though cattle and sheep were bred to some extent, but querns and grains of wheat are abundant; the cereals must have formed the mainstay of life. Secondly, neither tells (mounds), as in Hither Asia, nor immense cemeteries, as on the Nile, attest the prolonged occupation of the same site. Small clusters of huts with barns beside them are scattered very thickly all over the löss lands, but everywhere their occupation seems to have been relatively brief. In one instance it has been proved that barns were erected before dwellings. The explanation seems to be this: the crops being watered by rain and not by irrigation, the plots soon became exhausted. Thereupon, the land seeming unlimited, they were allowed to return to bush, and fresh plots cleared, till eventually, all the easily accessible land having been thus used up, the whole village was shifted to a new site at the centre of a fresh tract of virgin soil.

Societies that breed livestock as well as cultivating can counteract soil exhaustion by using the droppings of flocks and herds, and so avoid the wasteful nomadism imposed on the Danubians. The pastoral tribes of Western Europe seem to have discovered this solution even in neolithic times; the excavator of the hamlet of Robenhausen in Switzerland, himself a peasant farmer, observed between the human habitations the sites of cattle-stalls marked by thick accumulations of dung mixed with remains of the straw and rushes used as litter, and was able to infer that farmyard manure was deliberately collected. Though such positive evidence is not available, we may safely infer that the neolithic farmers of the Balkans, Greece and the East Mediterranean coasts generally adopted a like procedure, since tell-formation attests continuous occupation of the village sites.

All the principal species of animal now raised for food seem to have been domesticated already in the

Near East and Europe by societies still in the neolithic
stage. Only a few additions to the farmyard were
subsequently made by the importation of exotic
species—notably barnyard fowls that had been kept
in India during the third millennium, during the Iron
Age, while new breeds were evolved by crossing between local stocks and by selection. Similarly, Lowie
declares that every cultivable plant of any importance
has been discovered by preliterate societies. But
how old these discoveries were and where they were
made are less easy to determine, as vegetable remains
are seldom preserved in the archæological record.
Still, several species of wheat and barley and millet
can all be traced in neolithic sites. The neolithic
inhabitants of Switzerland cultivated in addition len-
tils, peas, carrots, and even apples, and used caraway,
linseed, and poppy-seeds as condiments. In Greece
and Macedonia people in the same stage grew figs
and pears too. And in the Near East dates, olives,
figs, grapes, sesame, onions, garlic, lettuce, marrows,
melons, beans, and peas helped to vary men's diet
before the bronze stage began.

Of course fruit-trees and vines that bear fruit year
after year tied their cultivators to the soil, discouraging
the nomadic habits displayed by the neolithic Danubians and contemporary pastoral tribes in Western
Europe. Indeed, the early emphasis on orchard husbandry, combined with the limitations on the water
supply to produce the sharp contrast between neolithic
societies in the Near East and their homologues in
Europe or in modern Africa. During historical
times the area of this sort of husbandry has been
steadily enlarged, while varieties of fruit and vegetable
have been spread as cultivated plants far beyond their
natural habitat.

Among pure cultivators (i.e., those who breed no
domestic stock) to-day women till small plots in
America and Oceania with a digging-stick (a pointed
stick, sometimes weighted with a perforated stone),
or in Africa with a hoe. Perforated stones like those

0491400

used to-day for weighting digging-sticks, found on neolithic sites in North Africa, may mean that the same implement was then used. The neolithic Danubians in Central Europe certainly used stone-bladed hoes. Wooden hoes are shown in use in Egypt in paintings from early historical times. But ere then, before 3000 B.C., a plough drawn by oxen or asses and guided by men had replaced the women with their hoes; agriculture—that is, the cultivation of *fields*—had been added to gardening—the tillage of small plots. Thereby not only was a heavy burden of toil shifted from women's backs, but the efficiency of tillage and the productivity of labour were substantially increased.

The new instrument being usually made entirely of wood till the Iron Age, its history can only be inferred from occasional pictures, or more rarely from ancient field boundaries. But its modern distribution is worth noting. Before the European expansion after A.D. 1500 the plough was used only in a zone extending from Europe and North Africa across Asia to China, with the exclusion of Siberia. Archæologically it is attested in Egypt and Mesopotamia before 3000 B.C., soon after in Cyprus, India, and Greece, and in China by 1300 B.C. Perhaps rather before the latter date it is depicted on rocks high up in the Italian Alps and in cave-shelters in Southern Spain, slightly later in Swedish rock-engravings. In England ancient fields indicate that no plough was used till late in the local Bronze Age, about 800 B.C., and then at first only in the south.

Early ploughs were relatively light implements that only scratched the ground. It was the custom in Italy to cross-plough each field, so the fields were made approximately square. This is, in fact, an adequate procedure in dry climates, but poorly adapted to the clay soils of England and temperate Europe. A heavier plough, drawn preferably by eight oxen, and equipped with a mould-board and coulter to turn over the sod, was accordingly devised. It was introduced into South-eastern England by an invading tribe, the Belgae of Julius Cæsar, and is attested on their territories not only by actual iron coulters, but also by long strip-fields that replace the older square ones.   The length of the field in each case was determined by the distance a team could comfortably travel without a breather, the rest interval being used for turning the plough.

Stockbreeding combined with plough agriculture enabled farmers to produce food above domestic needs.   The surplus could be employed to support craftsmen, traders, priests, and officials who did not grow their own food, and to pay for imported materials.   Excavations in the Near East show the villages of farmers turning into little townships that house in addition specialized craftsmen, that boast shrines as well as dwellings and granaries, and the inhabitants of which use foreign substances, notably metals.   Eventually, about 3000 B.C., in the great alluvial valleys of the Nile, the Tigris–Euphrates, and the Indus, the townships grow into cities, the shrines into temples.   The citizens include artizans, merchants, priests, officials, and even clerks.   A novel economic order has arisen; new classes have climbed on the backs of the peasantry; the historical period has begun; an economic revolution has been completed.   During the third and second millennia similar but rather smaller cities appear all over Hither Asia, in Crete, and lastly in Greece and on the Yellow River in China.   Meanwhile, even in the Western Mediterranean, in Cis-Alpine Europe, and the Iranian plateau, weapons and ornaments of bronze produced by specialized miners and smiths and distributed by professional traders were coming into general use.

The new Bronze Age equipment had at first little effect in increasing primary production; the amenities of civilization were in general reserved for townsmen or war-chiefs.   For the surplus produced by the peasantry was mostly absorbed and concentrated by gods and priesthoods, kings, or military aristocracies.

But in the Orient some of it was expended on reproductive public works, like canals, that extended the cultivable area and increased its yield. The new urban economy encouraged specialized farming for the market as against subsistence agriculture; that is, an individual farmer or a village, instead of trying to grow all the food required at home, could concentrate on the crop best suited to the local soils, say olives, and for corn and peas rely on bartering the surplus olives in the market. Particularly where the soil is diversified, as in Greece and Syria, the adoption of such a system should increase production, and the archæological evidence suggests that Palestine by 3000 B.C., and Crete by 2000 B.C., were exporting olive oil or wine to Egypt. Finally, trade or political expansion allowed of the acclimatization of new plants or animals in regions where they did not grow wild.

Otherwise it is unlikely that the new economy or bronze sensibly augmented the total food supply. They did not provide the farmer with more efficient metal tools. The peasants of Egypt and Palestine, as of Europe, still tilled the ground with the old " neolithic " ploughs and hoes of wood and reaped the grain with flint sickles. Only after 1500 B.C. do bronze sickles begin to figure in Egyptian pictures or European hoards. And bronze axes were too costly for large forest clearance.

Iron, on the contrary, made a great difference. About 1000 B.C. the farmers of Gerar, in Palestine, were already using iron hoe-blades, iron plough-shares, and iron sickles. Equipped with iron axes, European farmers, after 700 B.C., could seriously tackle the temperate forests. Improved methods of communication encouraged specialized farming and the diffusion of new crops and animals. Canal and drainage channels could be dug more easily with iron tools, so that substantial areas—for instance, in Italy— were opened up to cultivation. After 200 B.C. the work of the cultivator was lightened by the invention of irrigating machines worked by oxen to raise water from rivers and canals. But the evidence for these developments is almost exclusively literary, as is that relating to the even more striking innovations that began in the eighteenth century A.D. Though excluded from our programme, the results of the last are worth mentioning. According to the American President's Committee on Technological Trends and National Policy, 1937, " in 1787 the surplus produced by nineteen farmers was required to support one city-dweller; now nineteen farmers produce on the average sufficient to support fifty-six city dwellers and ten foreigners." It is most unlikely that the technological advances of the Iron Age, still less those of the Bronze Age, should have produced effects of that order, but the results of the neolithic revolution might be expressible in comparable figures were data available. On the other hand, the advances of the Iron Age have stood the test of time, inasmuch as the trends already traceable then have been maintained despite local interruptions. A visit to the " Dust-Bowl " suffices to inspire doubts as to how far large-scale mechanized farming will continue to be productive.

CHAPTER III

TOOLS, MACHINES, AND MATERIALS

THE enrichment of men's diet and enlargement of their food supply described in the preceding chapter, and indeed all extensions of human control over external nature, have been due to improvement in tools. For it is mainly with the aid of tools that men can act upon and alter the material world around them—their environment. Tools therefore provide a reliable index of the extent of men's independence of external circumstances, and archæologists are well advised in taking the technique of tool-manufacture as the basis of their classification.

The earliest tools were presumably merely natural objects, selected because they met an immediate need. In fact, the eolithic tools used by *Sinanthropus* at Chou-kou-tien are bits of quartzite that have been deliberately collected and utilized. But some eoliths even have been purposely chipped, the better to serve human ends. They look as if they had been made on the spur of the moment from some handy pebble for a particular purpose, as for instance when a hunter wanted to skin a buck he had just killed; after use such might be discarded. They would be *occasional* tools.

By the second interglacial men seem to have begun to provide themselves with tools deliberately made in advance. The irregular, unwieldy lump provided by nature was reduced to a handier shape by bashing it against a big fixed stone, a natural anvil. The product might be reduced to still more convenient proportions by secondary chipping with a rounded stone held in the hand as a hammer. The lower palæolithic tools thus produced can be divided into at least two great families, seldom found together, and rather differently distributed about the Old World. In one family, termed Clactonian, the most carefully made tools have been formed by chipping the edges of flakes detached by the anvil process. When all the suitable flakes that could be conveniently obtained had been knocked off the parent lump or core, the latter was discarded, though sometimes utilized.

In the other well-known family, termed Chellean-Acheulian, flakes were also utilized as tools. But the core itself was even more carefully treated, as if the main concern of Chellean and Acheulian men had been to reduce the core to a definite shape. The resultant core-tools are generally called *hand-axes*— rather unhappily, since they are ill-adapted for chopping. Indeed, no one knows precisely what they were used for; they might serve for cutting, scraping, digging, or even throwing. Actually they may have served a number of purposes, like the sailor's pocket-knife, as Sollas says. Hence they were not *specialized* tools. But they were *standardized*. All over the huge area where hand-axes are found— Western Europe, the whole of Africa, Hither Asia, and peninsular India—and throughout the 100,000 or 200,000 years of their currency, the same four or five shapes recur with surprising regularity. You can recognize a hand-axe by its form alone, whether it be made in flint, quartzite, basalt, or shale. This uniformity means that hand-axes were made to a pattern, or rather to one of several related patterns. Trial and error had convinced the social group that this or that shape was adapted to meet recognized needs. Social tradition approved and maintained the standard thus established. The individual no longer needed to think out on each occasion what sort of implement he had better make. His society gave him a model to copy, and doubtless taught him how to copy it. The model was of course quite concrete, visible, and tangible; the novice need not exercise very much foresight to see how to reduce a natural lump to the standard form. In the sequel the archæologist can recognize a cumulative increase in the skill with which hand-axes were manufactured, and consequent perfection in their form, but no really radical innovation.

On the other hand, in the manufacture of flake tools the Levallois technique, first perceptible just before the third ice age, marks an important advance; for it involves careful preparation of the core before tool-making proper can begin. Its object was to secure a nice thin flake of a standardized form (eventually the triangular flakes described as spearheads on p. 14). An area of the requisite shape was blocked out on the core by a series of well-directed preparatory blows, so that a suitable flake would come off preformed when the final blow was struck on a surface specially prepared to receive it. To do this the worker had in imagination to look ahead beyond the actual lump before him much further than an Acheulian or a Clactonian. To this extent the Levallois process presupposes greater powers of foresight, an advance in mental capacity.

Moreover, it is suitable primarily for the manufacture, in advance of actual need, of a stock of flakes. For it is an extravagant process, wasting a large part of each lump, and so can only be practised where raw material is plentiful. Finally the triangular Levallois flake or point became at last a more or less *specialized* implement. Anyone can see that it would make a splendid spearhead.

During the last interglacial period the separation between the two tool families seems to have broken down—the flake and core traditions seem to blend. But in European caves during the first phase of the last ice age (Würm I) we find a rather poorer industry, predominantly in the Clactonian flake tradition, associated with the skeletons of Neandertal men, a still very ape-like species.

The cave deposits contain two standardized tools in enormous numbers—a triangular-pointed flake trimmed along both edges and a D-shaped flake trimmed only along the convex edge. Both could be used as knives and scrapers, the point also as a

70857

spearhead. The Marxist prehistorian, Efimenko, suggests they were made for use by men and women respectively, like the man's knife and the woman's knife of the modern Esquimaux. They would then denote a differentiation of labour between the sexes.

But even earlier there are hints of another technical advance in the more genial climate round the Mediterranean; *blades* appear associated with late Acheulian hand-axes in Palestine and Spain. To produce them the core had to be prepared more carefully than even a Levallois core, till it assumed a cylindrical or prismatic form, with at least one flat end. Suitable blows on the latter would then detach a whole series of long, narrow, and thin flakes, for which the name *blade* is reserved. On blades were made secondary tools such as gravers for cutting bone and ivory.

A *secondary tool* is one designed not to satisfy immediate needs, like killing a buck, cutting it up, or skinning it, or even preparing its hide for use as clothing, but only for making other tools that shall better meet such primary needs. It is a tool for making tools. North of the Alps secondary and blade-tools are distinctive of all upper palæolithic groups, and appear together with the first skeletons of men like ourselves, members of the species *Homo sapiens*. And all recent representatives of that species, even the lowest known savages, the Tasmanians, had reached the stage of making blades and secondary tools. At the same time, in some regions and by some societies—for instance, the so-called Aterians of North Africa—blades and Levallois flakes were used concurrently during the upper palæolithic. Here, too, a new method of thinning down flakes by pressure instead of percussion first appears.

The upper palæolithic marks an industrial revolution. The capacity of *Homo sapiens* to shape the external world was greatly enhanced by a variety of specialized tools—flint knives with the backs blunted by trimming, precursors of our own table knives, and composite knives formed of several short blades

mounted in a single wooden handle, several kinds of
scraper, awls and piercing tools, gravers and small
saws suitable for cutting bones. With secondary
flint tools men could now make implements of bone,
antler, and ivory. Splinters carved from bones or
tusks were perforated with awls to make the first
needles. In piercing the needle-eyes or string-holes
for beads, a rotary motion was probably used, and
possibly a sort of drill. For shaping and sharpening
the new materials a new process, grinding and polish-
ing, was discovered; it was subsequently applied to
stone. Some upper palæolithic tools seem already
intended for wood-working—planes and choppers of
flint cores, and wedges, or even chisels of antler and
ivory with ground edges. Without these new tools
the improved hunting and fishing tackle described on
p. 15 and the snug houses to be mentioned on p. 45
would have been inconceivable.

The mesolithic relics most familiar to archæologists
are tiny flints termed *microliths*. They must have
been used to make composite tools and weapons by
an extension of the idea already applied in the upper
palæolithic knives. But at least in Northern Europe
the outstanding achievement of the period was the
provision of an effective kit of carpenters' tools
derived from the antler and ivory wedges that had
been used in Eastern Europe already during the last
ice age. By applying to stone the process of grinding used to sharpen them was produced the polished
stone *celt*—an axe or adze-blade or chisel tougher
and harder than any organic material would yield.
At the same time the celt was attached to the end of
a wooden handle if it was to be used as an axe-head
or adze-blade. But of course the handle could not
be fitted into a hole in the stone head, as with our
iron axe-head (perforated stone axe-heads are certainly found in Central and North European neolithic sites, but they seem too fragile for use in chopping); instead the celt was fitted into a straight or
hooked wooden shaft or into a mount or slieve of

antler, which was then fitted into or on to the shaft. Polished stone celts combined with simple wooden mallets provided the inhabitants of the North European forests with a quite efficient kit of carpenters' tools from which only the saw was missing. With it they could shape paddles and even sledge-runners, some of which have been preserved in Boreal peats. A stone axe will even fell a tree, but it is hardly durable enough for clearing any large area in a temperate forest.

The polished stone celt used to be regarded by archæological systematists as the type fossil of the neolithic phase. And it was of course used by most, but not all, neolithic societies for carpentry, as in mesolithic times. But it hardly seems sufficiently important to define a phase that is better characterized by the epoch-making development of food-production as explained on p. 12. And neolithic societies as thus defined generally had at their command other tools. Besides their hoes, sickles, and querns demanded by cultivation, most neolithic societies employed an efficient drill that could pierce thick blocks of tough stone that mesolithic peoples could perforate only by laborious hammering. The drill-stock was presumably of wood, and was probably rotated by looping a bow-string round it and then moving the bow backwards and forwards with one hand while the other pressed on the top of the stock. This is called a *bow-drill*, and remained in use till the Middle Ages, when it was slowly superseded by the brace. In neolithic times the bit might be of flint, or even of bone; but the actual boring was done by sand used as an abrasive. For boring a large hole some neolithic societies in Europe economized labour by using a tubular drill, probably of bone, that ground to powder only the circumference of a cylindrical section of the stone till it fell out on the completion of the operation. Other societies in Cyprus, Syria, Crete, and Egypt learned by using suitably shaped flint bits to hollow out vases in very hard rocks. Incidentally abrasives were used also for sawing up blocks of stone for the manufacture of celts and other utensils.

Moreover, neolithic societies, not content with helping actively in producing their own food supply, went on in the same aggressive spirit to manufacture substances not found as such in nature. Practically all neolithic societies had discovered the technique of making *pottery* (such mesolithic societies as practised the art may have learned it from neolithic neighbours). That is to say, they had discovered how, by application of heat, to convert clay, that when moist is completely plastic and that disintegrates with an excess of moisture, into a substance that is hard and resistant to the touch and unaffected by water. In technical language, they could induce a *chemical* change and break up the molecules of hydrated aluminium silicate, expelling the water of constitution to leave an anhydrous silicate.

To apply the discovery to the production of vessels they had also to learn the delicate and laborious processes of preparing the clay, building up the vessels slowly by hand, drying them, and finally firing them. Soviet experts have recently examined the fingerprints left by neolithic potters on their vessels; all belonged to women. Hence we may infer that, as is the rule among barbarians to-day who do not use the wheel, pot-making in the Stone Age was a female craft.

Secondly, wherever evidence is available, neolithic societies spun and wove. That is, by the rotary motion of the *spindle* they extracted long threads from flax or cotton or sheep's wool and wove these together into linen or cloth on a complicated mechanism termed the *loom*. Apart from actual textiles, the only archæological evidence for spinning is provided by little discs of stone or pottery used to weight the spindle, and termed *whorls*. Looms, being made of wood, have perished altogether. Illustrations from later archæological periods show three types—a horizontal loom, the earliest type used in Egypt, and two varieties of vertical loom. In one of the latter, best known in Europe, the warp-threads were weighted with perforated stones or lumps of clay that sometimes survive to prove the use of the device. The textile industry, too, on ethnographical evidence, should have been in the charge of women in neolithic, as in historical, times.

With the reserves of food placed at their disposal by the neolithic revolution, unidentified societies proceeded to make fresh discoveries and inventions to enlarge still further their control over brute nature. Small objects, like pins, of copper have been found in neolithic settlements like Sialk in Iran, and graves as at Badari in Egypt. These are made of native copper. Native copper must have been much commoner in the past; after 5000 years of prospecting and mining there is little left in the more civilized parts of the Old World. It is still found in the Matra Mountains of Hungary, and in Hungary and the Balkans large prehistoric implements of native copper have turned up in considerable numbers—particularly adze-blades, reproducing the shape of the Danubians' stone celt, and also axe-adzes, axe-hammers, and pick-axes, all with a hole for the shaft like our axe- and pick-heads. These Hungarian implements, like the pins from Iran and Egypt, have been shaped simply by hammering; the metal has been treated as a superior sort of stone that is tough as well as hard, and can therefore be bent and hammered into shapes not obtainable by chipping or grinding stone or cutting bone and antler. Men have discovered that metal is *malleable*. This stage is often termed the Copper or Chalcolithic Age. The native tribes of the Lakes area in North America got that far and stopped there.

Between 4000 and 3000 B.C. some society or societies in Hither Asia made the further discovery that copper is *fusible*: it becomes liquid when heated and can then be made to assume any desired shape, but on cooling it recovers all the desirable properties of a superior stone. *Metallurgy* may be said to begin with this discovery. In practice it seems as if copper-melting was coeval with copper-*smelting*—the production of the useful metal by heating certain crystalline stones or coloured earths with charcoal. This means the discovery of the chemical process of reduction, a transubstantiation much more startling than that controlled by the potter with her kiln, but of the same kind. As copper ores are very much commoner than native copper, smelting permitted a more extensive use of metal. But ores are generally found in barren mountainous country remote from the haunts of neolithic farmers or centres of urban population, and in the form of thin veins or lodes embedded in very hard rocks. At first only surface lodes were worked by open quarrying, as illustrated by the older workings in Sinai, Transcaucasia, the Eastern Alps and elsewhere. Though neolithic men mined for flint in the chalk, their methods and tools were of no avail in dealing with the hard, metalliferous rocks. Only after 1500 B.C. do we find evidence of copper-mining. The prehistoric mines at the Mitteberg in Upper Austria between 1200 and 800 B.C. illustrate a refined technique owing little or nothing to that of the neolithic flint-miners of the English Downs. And before the products of deep mining could be utilized, another discovery in metallurgical chemistry had to be made; for the deep ores, being generally sulphides, cannot be directly reduced by smelting with charcoal, but must first be oxidized by roasting in the air. Roasters have been found at the Mitteberg and near the Gulf of Akaba.

The utilization of the foregoing discoveries required a number of inventions—some sort of furnace, a blast, eventually supplied by bellows—to provide the requisite heat, crucibles to contain the molten metal, and moulds to give it the desired form.

Other metals were soon discovered. Silver and lead were known in Hither Asia before 3000 B.C., but neither was used in Britain till after 500, though Britain is well supplied with lead ores.   Metallic tin had been found in the village of Thermi on Lesbos soon after 3000, and about the same time an alloy of tin and copper—*bronze*—was being used in western Asia Minor, Mesopotamia, and the Indus valley. Bronze gives a more reliable casting than unalloyed copper, and eventually supplanted it as an industrial metal.   But down to about 1800 B.C. in Egypt, and 1000 years later in South Russia, only unalloyed copper was regularly employed.   Tin, it should be remembered, is very much scarcer than copper or even lead.   Nevertheless any period in which tools, weapons, and ornaments were regularly made by casting, whether of copper or of bronze, is traditionally termed a Bronze Age.

The metallurgy of copper or bronze provided opportunities for immense improvements in human equipment, since an infinite variety of shapes can be produced by casting, and limitations on size are largely overcome.   But the realization of their potentialities was restricted by the relative scarcity of the materials and the cost of transport from the metalliferous mountain regions to the fertile valleys where population naturally congregated.   Bronze Age objects turn up in abundance only in regions rich in ores, like England, Ireland, South-eastern Spain, Cyprus, and Bohemia, or where the supply was systematically organized, as in Mesopotamia, the Indus valley, and Egypt.   Everywhere metal was used in the first instance for weapons and ornaments.   Among the barbarian societies of Europe we find no metal tools, apart from a few adzes and chisels, till the Late Bronze Age.   The civilized societies of the Indus valley, Mesopotamia, Egypt, and the East Mediterranean were acquainted with a culinary service of bronze cauldrons, ladles, flesh-hooks, strainers, and drinking tubes, not to mention vessels; but such are found exclusively in temples or the houses of kings and rich nobles, and must have been extremely expensive. But these societies provided craftsmen with superior metal instruments for delicate work—saws, chisels, adzes, axes, nails, and gouges, drill-bits, specialized knives. But for rough work—hoeing, reaping, and other agricultural operations, tree-felling, quarrying, and dressing stone—the old neolithic equipment of wood and stone remained in use.

After 1500 B.C., presumably as a result of the development of mining and the discovery how to treat sulphide ores, metal became commoner everywhere. Even European barbarians could now afford to provide carpenters with bronze gouges, chisels, and adzes, smiths with light hammers, and small anvils of metal, miners with heavy bronze hammers and picks, and even some farmers with sickles. In the civilized Orient bronze hoe-blades and sickles became commoner. Even so, bronze never replaced stone in the way iron did.

Hence in themselves copper and bronze did not extend human control over nature anything like as much as might have been inferred from the revolutionary possibilities of the new materials. Such outstanding works of Bronze Age civilization as the irrigation and drainage of the alluvial river valleys on the one hand, the building of Egyptian pyramids and Mesopotamian temples on the other, could have been, and to a very large extent were, executed with a neolithic equipment. Doubtless the economic revolution which such works symbolize was accelerated, if not caused, by the imperious necessity of importing metal for armaments if society were to be preserved. Doubtless, too, its form was conditioned and its results consolidated by the power conferred upon temples, kings, or chieftains through the monopoly of such costly armaments. But that also prevented the use of the new material for more general betterment.

On the other hand, more delicate tools of metal increased the carpenter's mastery of woodwork. Even among barbarians in Europe the Bronze Age carpenter could make mortise-and-tenons joints, and so build better houses. It is arguable that a plough, being normally constructed of at least two pieces of wood firmly jointed together, could never have been produced without metal tools. (Its distribution coincides with that of the products of Bronze Age metallurgy.) The no less decisive invention of the wheel is more firmly connected with bronze equipment.

Applied to vehicles it revolutionized transport, and to that extent contributed to the rise of urban civilization. Even mesolithic societies in Northern Europe had used sledges to transport burdens over the snows; the same device had been used on steppe and desert in Hither Asia and Egypt. Before 3000 B.C. the sledge was mounted on wheels and became a cart or a war-chariot. Attested by pictures of that age in Mesopotamia we find the wheeled vehicle in India, too, by 2500 B.C., in Crete just after 2000, in Egypt not before 1600, and in Mainland Greece just after that date, in China and Sweden soon after 1400, in Britain not till 800. In Africa, south of the Sahara, in the Americas, in Australia, and Oceania, wheels were unknown till introduced by Europeans in modern times. Wheeled vehicles were of decisive importance for another reason. With the plough the cart is the first unambiguous indication of the use by man of non-human motive power. By shifting the burden of transport to the shoulders of the ox and the ass, men were taking the first step on the road to the modern use of power, and eventual emancipation from toil.

A second application of the wheel—to pottery—seems contemporary with the cart in Iran and Mesopotamia. By throwing on to the centre of a spinning disk a lump of clay, a specialized craftsman can produce in a few minutes a vessel that it would take a woman as many days to build up by hand. This labour-saving invention made pottery a specialized and mechanized industry—the first in human history.

The distribution of wheel-made pottery, which is

easily recognizable (actual wheels seldom survive), shows that the invention had reached India, Syria, and Palestine, and possibly Egypt, soon after 3000 B.C. It had spread the Asiatic shores of the Ægean shortly before 2000 B.C., but was not adopted in Crete till 1800, nor in Mainland Greece till 1600. China certainly knew the wheel by 1400 B.C., but in the Western Mediterranean vases were all hand-made till after 800, north of the Alps down to 250, in England till 50 B.C. and in Scotland till A.D. 400. In Ireland and Northern Europe the potter's wheel arrived still later, in the Americas and Oceania only after the wheeled vehicle with European colonists.

Some sort of *lathe* was known to the civilized societies of the Near East and India by 3000 B.C. and even to barbarians in England by 1600. Hence this application of rotary motion may be as old as the potter's wheel. Finally *sailing-ships* are first represented on some Egyptian monuments shortly before 3000 B.C., but they are boats foreign to the Nile, and probably coming from Asia. In any case by that date the power of the wind as well as the strength of oxen had been harnessed to man's service, and this time it is an inanimate motive power that man has started to control.

All the major inventions just considered were launched before 3000 B.C., before there were rich urban civilizations and states disposing of an accumulated surplus of real wealth anywhere in the world. It might have been anticipated that the urban revolution, which did at least secure to the crafts an adequate supply of raw materials, would have been followed by an outburst of chemical discoveries and mechanical inventions. Nothing of the sort happened. During the eighteen centuries of the Oriental Bronze Age the applications of former discoveries were certainly improved, some new substances and processes were discovered for the manufacture of ornaments and luxury articles (glass, cast and moulded but not blown, was the most important), but no new materials nor techniques to meet the needs of the great masses.

This industrial stagnation ended as soon as metal tools became cheap and plentiful with the Iron Age. Iron ores, often, indeed, of very low grade, are available almost everywhere. They can be reduced, like copper ores, by heating with charcoal. But at the temperature available without a mechanical blast, iron does not fuse, so smelting yields not a lump of pure metal, but a spongy mass of iron, charcoal, and slag that can be compacted into an ingot only by prolonged hammering and repeated heating. And to obtain any considerable quantities some sort of blast-furnace is required.

Now apart from ornaments of meteoric iron, small objects of terrestrial iron have been found in Mesopotamia and Asia Minor even before 2000 B.C. and more frequently in the succeeding centuries. The secret of iron-forging was accordingly known, and there are many grounds for supposing that it had been discovered and jealously guarded by some barbarian tribe in Armenia, where rich ores exist. Then after 1100 B.C. tools and weapons of iron began to be made in numbers, and locally first in Palestine–Syria, Asia Minor, and Greece, then in Mesopotamia and Iran, after 750 even north of the Alps, after 500 B.C. even in Britain and Northern Europe. The secret has been divulged and spread abroad. As a result metal became cheap and generally accessible for the first time. For that reason the Iron Age initiated an industrial revolution, even though iron weapons were, at least at first, inferior to the costly bronze ones.

Remains of slag and furnaces show that iron was smelted everywhere in villages and even isolated farms, whereas copper slags and smelting-ovens are found only on the mine-fields. So the rural population were no longer dependent for their supplies of metal on far-flung trade and costly transportation; Iron Age farmers could probably smelt iron for themselves in the slack winter season, as Swedish peasants still did last century, though first-class iron made from high-grade ores—those of Elba, for example—was still the object of extensive trade.

From this cheap metal peasants could make for themselves efficient agricultural tools. Right at the beginning of the Iron Age, at Gerar in Palestine, Petrie found iron hoe-blades, and even ploughshares, as well as sickles. Then cheap but durable iron axes made tree-felling practicable on a large scale; the barbarian tribes of Europe seriously began to clear the forests and so opened fresh land to cultivation. For the same end the marshes in Italy were drained by tunnels driven through hard rock with the aid of iron picks and gads, while in torrid desert countries like Iran spring-water for irrigation could be conducted without loss by evaporation through subterranean channels that only iron tools could cut. In the sequel the productivity of farms was greatly enhanced by new metal tools. Shears were invented somewhere about 500 B.C.—previously sheep had been plucked, not shorn. Before the beginning of our era Greek and Roman farmers were equipped with bill-hooks, pruning-knives, scythes (together with mowers' anvils for sharpening them in the field), pick-axes, mattocks, shovels, entrenching tools and spades with at least an iron sheath to the wooden blade.

Other crafts benefited in the same way. Before 500 B.C. Greek smiths were using several kinds of specialized metal hammers, anvils, hinged tongs, a variety of bits, rymers, and chisels and improved bellows. In Roman times we find also specialized nail-makers' anvils and blocks for wire-drawing. Similarly Greek and Oriental carpenters by 500 B.C. were using frame and cross-cut saws, as well as a great variety of hammers, axes, gouges, adzes, and chisels adapted to particular operations, and supplemented by 50 B.C. even with planes and augers. Other artizans, from shoemakers and masons to miners and quarrymen, were proportionately assisted.

Indirectly iron improved transport and the amenity of cities. Bigger and better ships and wagons could be built with plentiful iron tools and bolts; roads and bridges were constructed. Engineers with iron tools cut a tunnel $\frac{1}{3}$ of a mile long through a mountain to bring water to Samos before 500 B.C.

The astounding enlargement in man's control over nature due to iron tools was soon followed by measures for the reduction of toil through extensions of rotary machinery. For the cheapness of metal parts and of tools for wood-working and stone-cutting permitted the manufacture of fairly precise machines at no excessive cost.

The most decisive steps in this direction are observable in the building and flour-milling industries. The heavy lintels of Stonehenge among the barbarians of Bronze Age Britain, and the even heavier blocks of pyramids and temples in civilized Egypt, had been dragged into place up specially constructed ramps by brute human labour-power unaided by any mechanical devices. The same procedure was used for the colossal statues of the early Iron Age Assyrian kings (as their sculptures show) and for the pediments of temples in Asiatic Greece shortly before 500 B.C. (according to a rather late written account). But by 450 B.C. the Greeks were using windlasses, pulleys, and a sort of crane for raising such weights, and a capstan seems to have been invented about the same time. By the beginning of our era tombstones illustrate shears with block and tackle and scissors as good as ours.

Throughout the Bronze Age, in the greatest cities as much as in rural villages, each household ground its own flour from grain as some people grind their own coffee at home to-day, and home-milling remained the usual practice through much of the Iron Age too. Down to about 600 B.C. the grains were everywhere ground in a mortar or on a saddle-quern, pushed to and fro. The labour involved was enormously reduced thereafter by replacing the to-and-fro motion of the hand-rubber by the rotary motion of a circular grinder pivoted on the nether millstone by an iron staple through the centres of both. This machine is termed a *rotary quern*, and was still used in the Highlands a century ago, as it is in India to-day. A specimen from Syracuse, in Sicily, is said to be older than 500 B.C., a certain example from Olynthus, a Greek colony in Macedonia, may be a century later. After 300 B.C. rotary querns turn up frequently in the civilized cities of Greece, Italy, and North Africa, and among the barbarian Iberians in Spain, though still in competition with saddle-querns. North of the Alps the new machine appears among the Celts in Switzerland about 200 B.C., in Southern England after 100 B.C., and in Scotland after A.D. 80, but it is not found among the Teutons of the North till 200.

The invention of the rotary quern saved the house-wife, or her slaves if she had any, many hours of grinding toil. A contemporary application of the same idea in bakeries was to lift that burden from human shoulders altogether. As early as the fifth century bakers catering for the popular demands of Greek and Italian cities began to instal in their shops large mills constructed on the same general principle as the rotary quern, but of much greater size, and worked by a donkey walking round and round. Such represent the first extension of non-human motive-power since the invention of the plough, the ox-cart, and the sail in the fourth millennium. The earliest archæological evidence for the use of donkey-mills comes from the Semitic (Phœnician) colony of Motya in Sicily destroyed in 397 B.C., but after 300 complete specimens are quite common in Greek and Italian cities like Delos and Pompeii.

A similar machine seems to have been used for grinding ore, judging from one found in the silver mines of Laurion near Athens and probably older than 400 B.C. At the same time large mills of different construction, but also using rotary motion and driven by animal motive-power, came into use for crushing olives when, thanks to improved shipping, olive oil came to be produced on a large scale for a Mediterranean market. Parts of such a mill have been found at Olynthus, and must be older than 400 B.C.

The donkey-mill had been devised to meet the needs of the substantial middle-class population of a Classical city, and spread beyond the Mediterranean basin only after Alexander the Great and the Romans founded cities of Classical type. But about 100 B.C. a new mill in which water replaced the donkey as motive-power was invented. The evidence is at first exclusively literary, but it is clear that the machine involved gears. For, as in the quern and the donkey-mill, the millstones revolved in the horizontal plane, but the water-wheel naturally turned at right angles thereto. The wheel itself, with its vanes, the shaft, and even the greater part of the gears, were of wood, but the earliest literary reference, a short Greek poem, implies that metal buckets were at first used instead of vanes.

By reversing the action of a wheel of the last-mentioned type it could be used to irrigate fields or drain mines. Remains of such wheels have in fact been found in Roman mines in Spain. The wheels were turned by slaves, and it took a battery of two 14-foot wheels to give a lift to 10 feet 6 inches. The irrigating machines used in Egypt, however, were probably driven by a donkey or an ox walking round and round as if it were attached to a corn-mill, but actually turning not a millstone, but the vertical shaft meshed with the horizontal shaft carrying the wheel and buckets. This is the principle of the so-called Persian wheel still used for irrigation in the East to-day.

The donkey-mill and the water-wheel represent the highest mechanical achievement of the ancient civilizations and are as far as they ever got with labour-saving machinery and the relief of men from toil.

Significantly enough, very little use was made of the water-wheel till A.D. 400, when Roman civilization was collapsing. Yet upon it depended largely the advance to the modern machine age. In the Dark Ages water-mills for grinding corn spread rapidly in Europe; for this continent is blessed with plenty of permanent streams to drive them. By A.D. 800 they were being installed even in England. Then in the Middle Ages water-power was set to work pulping-mills (1290), bellows in blast-furnaces (1295), hammers in forges (1320), sawmills (1322), wire-drawing machines (1400), spinning-machines, etc. Cast iron (cf. p. 38) was one of the more important by-products of this extension.

The major manual tools with which men can shape their environment to their needs had all been perfected, or at least invented (the Romans, for example, had some sort of pump), in the Iron Age. The further extension of man's control over nature was very largely due to the fuller use of power-driven machines. Such were both the condition for producing the old familiar substances in bulk and newly discovered materials on an effective scale and the harness for novel sources of power. And so man's mastery of matter and annihilation of space in the twentieth century is just the consummation of a progressive process initiated by the eolithic tools several hundred thousand years ago.

CHAPTER IV

WARMTH AND SHELTER

Homo sapiens, Man, has a wider geographical range than any other animal species. He has colonized arctic tundras and tropical forests with equal success. His success in this respect is presumably due to his capacity for making himself an artificial environment and controlling the temperature of the air immediately around him through the use of fire and the construction of shelters.

The use of fire seems a distinctively human trait; wild animals are wont to flee in terror from its flames. Even the very early " eolithic" Pekin men who lived in a cave at Chou-kou-tien seemed to have at least cherished fire and utilized its heat for warmth, and perhaps for cooking, since bones from their cave have been burnt. Whether they knew how to kindle fire is much more doubtful. The fire-producing devices most generally used among recent savages are all based on the friction of two pieces of wood, and could not therefore figure in the archæological record. The first evidence for the deliberate production of fire comes from upper palæolithic times in Europe. In some Belgian caves inhabited during the last ice age have been found pieces of scratched iron pyrites together with flints blunted along the edges, as flints are after frequent striking against steels. When struck with a flint, iron pyrites gives a spark, just as steel does. So upper palæolithic Europeans had discovered the method of fire production used by their successors till the introduction of the phosphorus match in the nineteenth century. The only major advance in the interval was the substitution of metallic iron for its ores in the Iron Age.

Wood was of course the oldest, as it is still the commonest, fuel. The discovery of charcoal must be at least as old as copper-smelting (p. 33). Peat was burned in Orkney already by neolithic villagers. Coal exceptionally fed the flames of funeral pyres during the Bronze Age in Wales. It was employed rather more extensively for industrial purposes in Wales and North Britain during the Roman period, and in China even before the beginning of our era, but it could not be burned on domestic hearths owing to its poisonous fumes till a chimney had been invented.

In Central France, round the Pyrenees, and in the Crimea, capacious caves offered Neandertalers and more modern men shelter against the rigours of the last ice age. On the South Russian steppes, exposed to the full fury of polar gales, Gravettian hunters were able to take toll of the mammoth herds (p. 14) only because they could dig them shelters in the löss soil and roof them with skins or turfs, thanks to the equipment mentioned on p. 29. At Kostienki on the Don Soviet excavators recently uncovered such a palæolithic house, 113 feet long and 18 feet wide; a row of nine distinct fireplaces down the centre suggests that it was the communal abode of a group of nine families. Such subterranean dwellings, still occupied by Polar tribes, are comfortably snug, if rather stuffy and hard to clean. Very similar structures seem to have been inhabited by the neolithic Danubians in Central Europe, only they were rather smaller; a representative Danubian house measures 70 by 27 feet, and half-subterranean houses of smaller size adapted for one family only were still being constructed in Northern and Central Europe during Roman times and the Dark Ages.

But the perfection of carpenter's tools with the neolithic stage (p. 30) allowed farmers to build above ground shelters nearly as efficient and considerably more hygienic. In Central Europe and the Balkans neolithic houses were rectangular, built on a skeleton of stout, earth-fast posts supporting walls of wicker-work or split sapplings, plastered with clay and dung, and roofs probably of thatch, birch-bark, or turf.

Such houses might measure 32 feet long by 17 feet wide, and were often divided into a porch or ante-chamber and an inner room. They were heated by open hearths supplemented by ovens, which in the cold Ukraine might grow into regular stoves. The wall-plaster might be whitewashed or painted, while ornamental clay mouldings attached to the finials or door lintels survive from Serbia, Hungary, Transylvania, and Moravia. In Switzerland and Southern Germany such houses were raised on piles above the shallow waters along lake-shores, thus economizing agricultural land, providing defence against wild beasts and men, and simplifying spring cleaning.

In stony countries, at least where the local rocks break easily into flat slabs, houses were often built of stones laid in mud or dung as mortar and to exclude draughts. The village of Skara Brae in Orkney, still open to public inspection, illustrates the high standard of comfort attained by a society disposing of only a neolithic equipment. In size the houses range from 15 by 13 to 21 by 20 feet. Though each consists only of a single room, one or more tiny cells in the thickness of the walls open off it. Warmth and light were provided by peat, burned on a square central hearth, on either side of which were fixed against the walls spacious enclosures to serve as beds. In shelves and cupboards, built against the rear wall and let into the side walls above the beds, provisions, gear, and clothing could be stowed neatly away. Lintelled drains under the house-floors connecting with a system of built subterranean conduits carried off liquid refuse.

Of course this attractive picture has another side. The floor of one house, found exactly as it had been left by its occupants on their last precipitate exit, was littered all over with rubbish, gnawed bones, and broken shells; remnants of choice joints were found even in the beds. The atmosphere of stench and squalor in which the neolithic Orcadians habitually lived could be disgustingly revived owing to exceptionally favourable circumstances. It would be unfair to generalize this impression to apply to all prehistoric barbarians. I have excavated Iron Age houses in Scotland which were disappointingly tidy, and so poor in relics. But still later Viking houses were even filthier than Skara Brae, as the scales, bones, and even heads of fishes were added to the refuse encumbering the floors. Dirt and squalor were probably normal conditions in rural habitations of neolithic times, and often much later.

In the marshy valleys of the Nile and the Tigris, Euphrates reeds offered a convenient material for quite efficient shelters, but the evidence for reed huts is naturally in the main inferential. But in the arid zones effective walls could be built of compacted clay, now termed *pisé* or *adobe*. The earliest houses at Sialk (p. 17) were thus built. Later, *adobe* construction gave place to brickwork: lumps of clay were shaped in the hands or, rather later, in a wooden frame and dried in the sun. Even in the river-valleys brick soon superseded reeds for urban architecture. Units thus preformed offered new opportunities to architects; they almost suggested the true vault and the dome. Both these devices were used by bricklayers in Mesopotamia before 3000 B.C., whereas in masonry only false or corbelled vaults were anywhere employed before the Iron Age. In wetter climates, like Assyria and Sindh, bricks could be made as resistant to moisture as stone by baking in a kiln, provided fuel were available. In firing bricks, of course, man is making a new artificial substance, related in its chemical composition and method of manufacture to pottery that had been discovered long before. This new substance was in use in Mesopotamia before 3000 B.C., and before 2500 whole cities were being built of kiln-fired bricks in India. By 1600 B.C. even tiles were being used for roofs in Greece.

So all the essential materials employed by peasant architects had been discovered by 3000 B.C. and

utilized to secure not only adequate shelter for man
and beast, but also a certain modicum of comfort.
In fact, rural housing has seen no radical improvement since the Stone Age, save in so far as urban
adaptations have percolated to the countryside. A
Hebridean "black house" of the nineteenth century
A.D. was scarcely warmer, lighter, or more sanitary
than an Orcadian house of the nineteenth century
B.C., and only slightly larger.

Urban housing, on the contrary, has grown steadily
better since city life began, though perhaps only a
minority of the townsfolk have benefited by the improvements. To understand what that means, however, we must explain what a city denotes physically
to the archæologist, and therefore consider not
isolated houses, but their assemblage into groups.

The food-quest, tool-making, and the other human
operations that have provided archæologists with
their material, were, and still are, social activities
normally conducted by organized groups acting in
co-operation. At least the primary nucleus of individuals who are thus co-operating regularly must
dwell together in space. The size and structure of
the bands whose collective drives after mammoths
were so successful in South Russia (p. 14) may be
inferred from the large communal houses, each suitable for a small clan, of which two were exposed at
Kostienki (p. 45). In neolithic Europe the unit
co-operating in agricultural work is represented as a
rule by a cluster of from eight (Skara Brae) to thirty-
five (Ukraine) houses, on an average about twenty-one,
scattered over an area of 6 acres or less. At Skara
Brae the individual houses were connected by covered
alleys or passages, on the marshes of Switzerland and
Würtemberg by corduroy roads. As these streets
symbolize the social solidarity of the several households, so the fences or ramparts that surround some
of the villages, by cutting them off from raw nature,
create a distinctively human environment for the
villagers within their shelter.

In Egypt the neolithic village of Merimde, covering about 6 acres, might represent a cell of comparable magnitude, though neither the number nor the areas of individual houses were determined. In Greece and Hither Asia the necessity of living close to one of the rare springs or perennial streams may have favoured rather larger aggregations. There, in fact, the ruins of a barbarian village or township appear at first as a maze of small chambers divided into blocks by narrow, crooked lanes. As only the wall foundations survive, it is seldom possible to tell how many chambers belong to a single house, and consequently how large such a house was. Nor is the total area of any neolithic village in this region yet known. All were probably quite small; even after 3000 B.C., in the Bronze Age, the walls of Troy on the Dardanelles enclosed only an acre and a half! But, being closely built up, such villages would accommodate more people than the dispersed villages of Europe or Lower Egypt. The size of the unit that could permanently co-operate was in fact rigidly limited by the area from which food supplies could be effectively collected to support the component population. In practice most barbarian villagers must be supported by the produce of fields, within walking distance of the settlement, which they cultivated themselves.

The term " Urban Revolution " is graphically justified by the physical size of the new units— cities—that symbolize its consummation. Soon after 3000 B.C. the walls of Erech, in Mesopotamia, enclosed an area of 2 square miles, including, of course, orchards, gardens, and temples. Ur covered 220 acres about 2500 and Assur 118 before 2000. Mohenjo-daro, in India, about 2500 B.C., seems to have occupied a full square mile. Even though these areas included orchards, gardens, open spaces, and temples, the cities must have housed a population considerably larger than could be fed from fields cultivated by the citizens themselves. They must, that is, have drawn on supplies that only the Bronze Age improvements in transport mentioned on p. 36 could make available at one centre.

The location of the great Bronze Age cities on navigable rivers or canals incidentally emphasizes the importance of water transport. Even in the second millennium other less conveniently situated Bronze Age settlements, that must rank as cities, or at least townships, on the strength of the trade, manufactures, and even literacy attested by the relics, are still ridiculously small: Megiddo, in Palestine, covered $3\frac{1}{3}$ acres; Gurnia, in Crete, though containing sixty houses, measured superficially only $6\frac{1}{2}$ acres; the walled area at Mycenæ, the richest town in Greece, not more than 12 acres! But Carchemish, on the Euphrates in Syria, covered 244 acres about the same date.

In the Iron Age the old Oriental capitals grew to much greater proportions. About 700 the walls of Khorsabad, in Assyria, the capital of Sargon II, enclosed some 740 acres, including of course parks and gardens; Nineveh, in the next century, perhaps 1800 acres. The 11 miles of wall round Babylon a little later denote a still greater metropolis. But the outstanding fact is the growth of cities in Greece and the multiplication of similar cities round the Mediterranean and in Italy. Even before 500 B.C., Samos, with its parks, attained an area of 400 acres. In the next century the walled areas of the Greek colonies in Southern Italy and Sicily vary from 70 acres (Selinus) or 150 acres (Megara Hyblæa) to 605 acres (Locri) and 691 (Croton), with Gela, 260, near the average. Then in Roman times, while the Empire's capital reached 3,040 acres, even the recently civilized provinces of France and England were dotted with substantial cities—Autun, 490 acres; Treves, 700 acres; London, 300 acres; even Caerwent, 44 acres.

From the first some urban houses were more commodious than any barbarian farm; they cover larger areas and are divided into a greater number of distinct rooms. Moreover, in turning into a city the township, restricted spatially by its walls and its water supply, tended to grow upwards as well as outwards like New York. The flat roof, appropriate to the brick architecture of the arid zone of Hither Asia, could easily be turned into a second storey. Even in the third millennium town houses on the Indus, the Euphrates, and probably the Nile, were normally two-storeyed. Before 1500 B.C. such were being built at Knossos, in Crete. A thousand years later they were normal all over Greece and Italy. Of course nothing remains of the upper storeys to show their size or plan, and the following figures and descriptions apply to the ground floors only.

Most Oriental houses were built round a central court in the Bronze Age and subsequent periods down to the present day, and it is generally included in the overall dimensions given here. In India, about 2500 B.C., even a small house at Mohenjo-daro might measure 30 by 27 feet, and many were twice that size. About the same date a house at Opis (Khafaje) measured and comprised ten rooms, apparently all on one floor. But some five centuries later a typical two-storeyed bourgeoise house at Ur covered 40 by 33 feet, the central court being 16 feet square.

The table on p. 55 indicates the progress of housing in so far as it is measurable in superficial areas. The spacial enlargement naturally made possible a multiplication of apartments and the separation of rooms for cooking, living, sleeping, and storage. Size cannot indicate the addition of amenities strange at first to rural habitations. But all the better-class houses in the Indus cities have specially constructed bathrooms in the third millennium. In contemporary and later Mesopotamian cities such are not so universally conspicuous. In the smaller townships of Bronze Age Crete and Greece, bathrooms would seem to have been still luxuries confined to palaces. But in Classical Greece several houses at Olynthus boast bathrooms before 400 B.C., and Roman mansions have magnificent bathing facilities; for poorer citizens a multitude of well-appointed public bathing establishments were available, the ruins of which form a conspicuous feature in any Roman city, as in the camps of Roman legions. Latrines with quite comfortable seats have been found in some Indian and Mesopotamian houses of the third millennium, and were provided even in the subterranean sepulchral houses of contemporary Egyptian nobles.

Heating of urban dwellings made less rapid progress, for the second storey introduced complications. Braziers burning charcoal that gives off no smoke were sufficient for the short winters of India, Mesopotamia, Egypt, and Crete, although 10° or more of frost may be experienced at Baghdad for several weeks. But in the new Iron Age cities of Greece and Italy, despite the much colder climate, the same imperfect device was used throughout the Classical period, and indeed till to-day; for the fixed hearth that had warmed Greek houses of the Bronze Age was abandoned in the Iron Age. At Olynthus, in chilly Macedonia, some houses have fixed fireplaces, but only in the kitchens; the smoke escaped through a sort of flue or clerestory in the ground-floor walls. True chimneys have, indeed, been found in the well-preserved ruins of Pompeii, but apparently only in bakeries or similar industrial establishments.

But during the last centuries before our era an ingenious system of central heating was devised, originally for public baths. Heated air was made to circulate under floors that were raised on brick pillars, and later through hollows in the walls too. After 100 B.C. rich Romans were applying this *hypocaust* system to heating their dwellings in the metropolis and provincial cities too, and even the manor-houses (villas) on their country estates. Then, thanks to the hypocaust, they were able to face the horrors of a winter on the Rhine, the Seine, or even the Thames!

At the same time the introduction of mica or even heavy glass windows made it possible to exclude draughts and still admit some daylight. But hypocausts were confined, owing to the fantastic costs of construction and maintenance, to millionaires' mansions. It was improvement of the peasants' stove, and later the brick chimney and cast-iron grate, that made the winters bearable to North European citizens in the Middle Ages.

Any house to some extent isolates its inhabitants from the external environment and provides them with a humanly controlled climate to live and sleep in. The development of urban housing reflects the greatest progress achieved in extending this control over temperature and improving it. But the town house is only part of a larger environment that is itself deliberately moulded to suit human needs. Indeed, even villagers in the neolithic stage cooperated to adapt the external world to their needs. The families living at Skara Brae, in Orkney, buried the whole settlement in an artificial hill by heaping peat-ash, dung and refuse against the walls of their separate houses and over the roofed passages that connected them, and draining the whole complex with artificial channels. Bronze Age citizens adapted the landscape to social needs on a grander scale by building artificial islands of brickwork and digging wells, drainage channels, and water-courses.

A magnificent system of covered sewers and vaulted subterranean conduits drained Harappa and Mohenjo-daro in the Indus valley before 2100 B.C. (4000 years later New Delhi lacked any sort of sewerage system!). Some Mesopotamian cities, like Eshnunna, were as well served, but Assur, the first capital of Assyria, remained without drains throughout its long history. In the removal of refuse liquids a Bronze Age city—or even Skara Brae—was not so far short of modern standards, and it is superfluous to describe later links, such as the well-known and very ancient sewers of Rome. The supply of water had been less satisfactory. In the Indus valley, indeed, there were one or two wells in each block sunk to tap the subsoil waters of the plain. But in Egypt and Mesopotamia the average citizen must have had to fetch water, of doubtful purity, from the river or canal on which any city stood.

Fresh spring-water conveyed by aqueducts or tunnels was the gift of cheap iron tools. Sargon II of Assyria, about 720 B.C., built an aqueduct to bring water to the new palace and town he founded at Khorsabad, among the hills above Mosul. Before 500 B.C. engineers cut a tunnel a third of a mile long through a mountain to supply Samos. An aqueduct built before 300 to serve Rome carried the water through 10 miles of tunnels and over valleys on arches. In the classical Greek cities the water had still to be carried home from public fountains, but by the beginning of our era, at Rome, Pompeii, and other cities, water was already laid on to some private houses. The reader should remember that at this date a Briton in his hill-top town at Maiden Castle or Traprain Law was lucky if he had even a single well or spring within the ramparts. Often his women had to fetch the water every day from some stream or pool at the hill's base, as Algerian women do to this day.

So from the Bronze Age city in the Orient a line of development can be traced quite clearly over 5,000 years to the modern American city with its water, sewage, lighting, and transport services and its skyscrapers protected by air-conditioning from heat and dust as well as cold and damp. The progress attained is no less clear. It is only needful to insist again that it has been conditioned on the one hand by the technical advances indicated in Chapter III, on the other by economic and social changes that archæology can only infer, but that history can observe. These, too, must be regarded as on the whole progressive on the strength of the available archæological evidence.

SIZES OF SETTLEMENTS AND DWELLINGS.

NEOLITHIC VILLAGES, EUROPE

	HOUSES.		SETTLEMENT.	
	AREA, FT.	ROOMS.	NUMBER OF HOUSES.	AREA, ACRES.
Köln-Lindental (Rhineland)	70 × 27	Communal house	27	6¼
Skara Brae (Orkney)	{ 21 × 20 { 15 × 13	One room with cells	8	—
Aichbühl (Würtemberg)	32 × 17	Two rooms	19	·—

BRONZE AGE TOWNSHIP, CRETE

Gurnia (about 1500)	40 × 30		60	6¼

CITIES

DATE, B.C.	CITY.	TYPE OF HOUSE.	AREA, FT.	FEATURES.	AREA OF WHOLE CITY, ACRES.
2500	Mohenjo-daro, S.	Small house	30 × 27	Two-storeyed	600
		Large house	97 × 83	Two-storeyed	
	Khafaje ?, M.	? High priest's house	88 × 75	12 rooms round court 33 × 29	—
	Eshnunna, M.	Prosperous house	46 × 39	11 rooms, no central court	—
2300	Eshnunna, M.	Prosperous house	69 × 46	12 rooms not counting out-house and court	—
	Eshnunna, M.	Ruler's palace	230 × 85	36 rooms and courts	—
2000	Assur, M.	Large house	97 × 72	10 rooms round court	118
	Ur, M.	Prosperous house	40 × 33	7 rooms round court 18 × 16	220
1400	Akhetaten, E. (Amarna)	Prosperous house	73 × 68		—
1200	Assur, M.	Prosperous house	87 × 73	10 rooms	156
600	Babylon, M.	Prosperous house	98 × 82	19 rooms round court	—
350	Olynthus, G.	Prosperous house	85 × 56		220
200	Priene, G.	Modest house	26 × 20	3 rooms, two storeys	99
		Rich house	100 × 52	10 rooms	
50	Pompeii, I.	Prosperous house	108 × 108	12 rooms	150

S. = Sindh (India); M. = Mesopotamia; E. = Egypt; G. = Greece; I. = Italy.
▶ *Note.*—Save for the " High Priest's house," at Khafaje, all the above might belong to ordinary members of the bourgeoisie; palaces are of course enormously larger; that of Akhenaten, at Amarna, measured 426 × 324 ft., and that of Sargon II, at Khorsabad, stood on an artificial platform 45 ft. high that covered 25 acres!

CHAPTER V

INTERCOURSE AND THE DIFFUSION OF CULTURE

THE inventions and discoveries, the contrivances and devices, described in the last three chapters were each and all created and developed by distinct human societies taking advantage of the opportunities and materials offered by the various regions they severally inhabited and to meet the specific needs imposed by the peculiarities of the climates and other external circumstances to which they were exposed. Archæologists can distinguish at any time a multitude of distinct human societies by their different " cultures." But a culture is precisely the sum total of the weapons, tools, houses, vehicles, and other things of the sort just examined that were used by a single people. Cultures and their constituents are thus strictly comparable to the bodily " adaptations to the environment " that distinguish varieties and species of animals from one another. But such adaptive variations, established by natural selection as favourable to the species' survival, can be transmitted from one member of the species to another only by the physiological act of conjugation—that is, from parents to children.

The human adaptations considered in this book, on the contrary, can be transmitted from one individual to another of the same age group simply by precept and example. There is thus formed in our species " a cumulative tradition and a new form of heredity," as Julian Huxley puts it. What is even more remarkable, this cumulative tradition is not necessarily confined to any group of persons, related by blood, or even inhabiting the same locality. Mountain hares cannot transmit their variable coats to lowland hares which may dwell at the foot of their mountains; for by the time the peculiar adjustment to their mountain habitat has been established by natural selection they have become too different from lowland hares for effectual interbreeding. But a few people who had learned to cultivate grasses growing wild on their steppes, can impart the technique to the inhabitants of river valleys where no such grasses grow spontaneously, provided of course they bring the seeds with them. In other words, human experience can be pooled.

The process of pooling is technically called *diffusion*. In modern times it is easy to trace and prove the diffusion of an invention like the steam engine, thanks to abundant written documents. In the same way the diffusion of religious systems, like Mohammedanism, Christianity and Buddhism, can be traced almost as certainly, and in nearly as full detail, over very much longer periods. But when the evidence is wholly archæological, diffusion can seldom be established with the same precision. If the evidence is of a durable kind and a reliable chronological framework is available, something very near proof can be advanced. The condensed accounts given above of the distribution in space and time of wheeled vehicles, the potter's wheel, and the rotary quern, were designed to suggest that these inventions had in fact been diffused from rather vaguely defined centres. Alphabetic writing and coinage would have provided still more convincing examples. On the other hand, how far metallurgy was diffused from a single centre is much more debatable. At the moment a really independent time-scale for the early Bronze Age is lacking; the dates usually assigned to the beginning of the Bronze Age in illiterate lands like Northern Europe assume that it was later than in the centres of historical civilization—Mesopotamia and Egypt. Moreover, bronze was worked in pre-Columbian Peru, while the other devices mentioned are confined to a definite zone in the Old World.

Hence a controversy still rages between evolutionists and diffusionists. The former maintain that, owing to the general uniformity of human minds, any society at the appropriate stage of technological, economic, and social development will make the same discovery, provided of course the opportunity be present. Diffusionists contend that each major invention was historically made but once, and class as such metallurgy, pottery, " agriculture," the axe, stone-polishing, the bow, etc. Archæology cannot resolve this controversy.

But it can sometimes prove at least that opportunities for diffusion did occur, that intercourse did go on between distinct societies and widely separated regions. The discovery of substances like marine shells or minerals where they do not occur in nature and could not be brought by natural forces, or of manufactured goods far from the known point of fabrication, affords indisputable proof of intercourse in this sense; for the substances and articles must have been transported by men. In the archæological record an ever-growing variety of materials have demonstrably been thus transported with increasing frequency over greater and greater distances.

Obviously the transfer of material objects involves the movement of human beings from place to place, and so does the diffusion of ideas. Movement may mean *migration* when an organized human group founds a new settlement in a strange land, or " trade " when only isolated individuals or families travel. Both processes are agents in diffusion. The steam engine was spread in Africa mainly by conquest and colonization, in Japan or Russia entirely by trade. The diffusion of Mohammedanism was effected largely by migrations of Arab warriors, of Christianity and Buddhism largely by the efforts of individual missionaries. Both processes were presumably as active in prehistoric as in historic times. But the purely archæological evidence for migration is often highly ambiguous. We shall confine ourselves first to the less debatable domain of " trade " as demonstrated by actual transfer of identifiable objects.

Moreover, in amassing evidence for trade, archæologists are disclosing one decisive factor in the economic
revolutions that delimit the major phases in human
history. The urban revolution transformed the self-
sufficing village of barbarism into a city symbol of
civilization, when—at least for armaments—imported
bronze became indispensable for survival and the
supply was accordingly organized. The Industrial
Revolution rests upon a world supply of food-stuffs
to support the manufacturing population and a world
market to consume mass-produced commodities.

Of course the " trade " that archæology can detect
may cover all sorts of exchanges, including the free
interchange of gifts between kinsmen or friends, the
activities of itinerant merchant-craftsmen like modern
tinkers, and even the settlement of merchants or
artizans in a foreign city as English merchants settle
in Istanbul or American technicians in Magnitogorsk.

Trade in one of these senses goes back at least to
upper palæolithic times. During the last ice age
shells from the Black Sea or even the Mediterranean
coasts were being conveyed at least 500 miles to
camps on the middle Dnieper, and cowries from the
Gulf of Lions to the cave-dwellers in the Dordogne.
The traffic may not have been restricted entirely to
ornaments (that were in any case also magic talismans); a few of the implements found at Gagarino
in the Ukraine have been made from the kind of flint
that is found only 50 miles further down the Don
near Kostienki where there was a second camp of
Gravettian mammoth-hunters. In the Dordogne the
bones of sea-fish are not uncommon among the refuse
of the reindeer hunters' feasts. That might indicate
more or less regular exchanges between inland and
coastal Magdalenian tribes. Again, in mesolithic
Europe Mediterranean shells were brought as far as
Bavaria and the Upper Rhine, while Antrim flint
was used in Kintyre on the opposite side of the
narrow but stormy channel.

Barbarian societies were still less isolated from one

another.　The neolithic farmers of the Fayum procured shells for necklaces from both the Mediterranean and the Red Sea.　A little later the predynastic inhabitants of the Nile valley began to secure
regular supplies of malachite from Sinai for painting
their eyes.　Stones like turquoise, found in the neolithic villages of Sialk in Iran and Anau in Turkmenia,
illustrate the same sort of traffic.　Throughout the
Danube basin, and even beyond it on the Elbe, the
Saale, and the Middle Rhine (as well as in the Balkans),
Spondylus shells were commonly used for bracelets
and beads by Danubian peasants, though they had
to be brought from the Mediterranean.

In the later neolithic and chalcolithic phases imported materials were used not only for ornaments,
but also for utensils, though of course only side by
side with local products.　Obsidian—a volcanic glass
that is better than flint for the manufacture of knives
and arrowheads—must have been much sought after.
It occurs in nature in Abyssinia, Armenia, the Taurus
Mountains, on Melos in the Ægean, and the Lipari
Islands off the coast of Italy, and near Tokay in
Hungary.　But obsidian implements have been found
in early predynastic graves in Egypt, in the oldest
settlements on the Tigris–Euphrates delta, and in
neolithic villages in Assyria, Crete, Thessaly, Serbia,
Moravia, and Silesia.　In the same way especially
good or nice-looking flint was " traded " over wide
areas—banded flint from Galicia to Hungary and
Central Germany, yellow flint from Grand Pressigny
in the Loire basin to Jersey, Brittany, Switzerland,
and Belgium.

Similar observations have been made with respect
to the rocks used for the manufacture of saddle-
querns and axe-heads.　The Danubian peasants
round Liège on the Meuse sometimes ground their
grain on querns made from a rock quarried near
Mayenne on the Moselle.　And even pots were transported down the Rhine from the Main valley to
Cologne.

Even within the framework of a neolithic self-sufficiency there was room for some intercommunal specialization, and trade might furnish a livelihood supplementary to, if not in place of, that earned by personal farming or hunting. On the slopes of Penmaen Mawr in North-west Wales axes were turned out in a regular factory from a local rock. Its products have been recognized by petrologists in Anglesey and Wiltshire. On the Sussex Downs, as in East Anglia, Belgium, France, Portugal, Sicily, Egypt, and Galicia, small communities engaged in mining for flint, digging shafts to the best nodule-bearing bed and galleries along it with only antler picks, stone chisels, and bone shovels. Products of the Sussex mines turn up along the Thames. The flint-miners must have lived partly by bartering their winnings for meat and wheat raised by neighbouring communities. In neolithic villages in Rumania we find groups of flint blades, quite fresh, as if for sale. On the northern fringe of the Danubian province in Germany hoards of stone celts have been dug up that seem, like the bronze hoards mentioned below, to represent the stock-in-trade of travelling merchants. Naturally copper was handled in the same way. Axe-adzes of hammered copper such as are very abundant round the lodes of Slovakia and Transylvania turn up sporadically in the Ukraine, Silesia, and Lower Austria far from any ores.

Till the Bronze Age, however, trade was confined to luxuries. Mammoth-hunters in the Ukraine could live without Black Sea shells. The Danubians on the Meuse could have ground their grain on local stones, though they might then have eaten more sand with their porridge. The predynastic Egyptians may have thought malachite indispensable for decency, but they could have survived without it. But at least for weapons, metal became essential as soon as other societies were using it, since stone weapons are no match for metal ones. And save for the lucky few who lived over a copper-mine, the essential metal had to be imported. The Bronze Age may be said to begin in any region when its inhabitants have recognized that imported metal is a necessity at least for self-defence, and have organized their economy to secure a constant supply. Regular commerce begins in the metal trade.

A simple form is illustrated in barbarian Europe. North Italy, the whole of Central Europe from the Vistula to the Meuse, and the North as far as Denmark and Southern Sweden, were supplied with copper mainly from Hungary, the Eastern Alps, and the Saxon Erzgebirge, and with tin from the Saxon–Bohemian mountains; the British Isles, Brittany, and Northern France, on the other hand, from Irish and Cornish lodes. Each of these two provinces formed a commercial system whose parts were linked together by perambulating merchant-artificers like travelling tinkers. If the find-spots of bronze axes or daggers be plotted on maps, they are seen to lie along well-defined trade routes.

The very discoveries that mark these routes prove how hazardous the traffic was; they consist largely of hoards comprising numerous bronze articles, and each supposed to represent the stock-in-trade of a travelling merchant, hurriedly buried in a moment of danger. Each hoard left for archæologists to find stands for a merchant who has lost his life or at least his livelihood! No wonder bronze was costly. The two systems named were not unconnected. A number of British axes, daggers, and spear-heads have been found in Central Europe, and some Central European ornaments in England.

The traffic was not confined to bronzes. For instance, amber, first from Jutland and then also from East Prussia, was bartered by the Northerners for bronze. Amber beads are common all along the trade routes of Central Europe in hoards as well as graves, and reached Upper Italy, Greece, and Crete (about 1500 B.C.). Similarly Irish gold was exported to Britain, the Continent, and even Crete. In revenge a few Mediterranean manufactures in the shape of fayence beads have been found in Hungary, Holland, England, and Spain.

But it was the societies cultivating the great alluvial plains of the Nile, the Tigris–Euphrates, the Indus, and the Yellow River, who came to depend most completely on imports, and therefore developed commerce first and most highly. For these plains, though eminently fertile, lack not only all metal ores, but also good building timber—Mesopotamia and Sindh lack even stone for querns, celts, and buildings. On the other hand, the rivers offer a convenient means of cheap transportation. This dependence on imports may indeed be a principal reason for the precocious rise of the new urban economy in just these regions. In any case the furniture recovered from early tombs or buildings of the third millennium presents a formidable list of imported materials—in Egypt including copper from Sinai, gold from Nubia, cedar-wood from Lebanon, lapis lazuli from Afghanistan, marble from the Ægean islands; in Mesopotamia, besides copper and tin, silver and lead from Asia Minor, lapis lazuli, śank shell from peninsular India; in Sindh deodara wood from the Himalayas, śank shell, jade from Burma.

Trade was naturally not confined to raw materials, though to the archæologist these are the surest index of its extent. Seals of the type fashionable in Mesopotamia about 3000 B.C. have come to light in Central Asia Minor and the Greek islands; Egyptian stone vases, equally old, in Crete and Northern Syria. Most surprising of all, fifty or more seals, made in the cities of the Indus valley, as well as other Indian manufactures—even pots—have been dug up from the ruins of Ur, Umma, Kish, and Eshnunna, in Mesopotamia, from layers dated between 2600 and 2100 B.C. In the light of them, certain seals and toilet-sets found in the Indus cities may confidently be accepted as copies of Mesopotamian imports. These two primary civilizations were certainly exchanging goods—and so presumably ideas—quite actively during the third millennium!

Active and widespread though trade was in the Oriental Bronze Age, it exhibits one striking peculiarity: apart from metals, objects of long-distance trade that can alone be recognized were almost entirely luxury articles—precious materials for the cult of gods or departed monarchs, for the furniture of palaces and temples, and personal ornaments of small bulk. And of course metal itself, though imported into Mesopotamia in sufficient quantities to provide the militia with weapons and armour too, and rich citizens with cauldrons and buckets, was, as indicated on p. 34, used rather sparingly. There is very little archæological evidence for long-distance trade in cheap articles suitable for popular consumption. Still, dried fish was brought to Mohenjo-daro in Sindh from the Arabian Sea a couple of hundred miles away. This peculiarity partly conditioned, partly was conditioned by, the economic and social structure of Bronze Age civilization in the Near East and later on in China.

During the third and second millennia cities multiplied in Hither Asia and the East Mediterranean; each being a commercial centre, the volume and range of trade grew steadily without, however, losing its luxury character. Only among the maritime cities did more popular goods begin to circulate by virtue of the simplicity of transport by sea. Soon after 2000 B.C. pottery vases were exported from Crete not only to Mainland Greece, but also to Cyprus, Syria, and Egypt. They were at first handsomely painted vessels, and doubtless contained superior brands of oil or wine; they have, in fact, been found in nobles' tombs. Still, pottery is a substance suitable for mass production, and therefore at least capable of becoming cheap. In fact, after 1500 B.C. " Mycenæan " pottery from Crete, Greece, and especially Rhodes, was exported in quite large quantities to Egypt, Palestine, Syria, Cyprus, the coastal towns of Asia

Minor and Macedonia, and even Southern Italy and Eastern Sicily. Broken Mycenæan vases and some Egyptian pictures of Phœnician traders in Nilotic villages are the first indication of foreign trade in anything like popular consumption goods.

In the Iron Age the general increase in production and improvement in means of transportation and communication due to cheap metal tools are reflected alike in the volume and the range of trade. In the contracting barbarian fringe of civilization even during the first half of the Iron Age, the Hallstatt period, bronze cauldrons, buckets, and cups, manufactured in Upper Italy, reached Central Europe, France, Denmark, Southern Sweden, and the Ukraine, while amber flowed back along the old trade routes in unprecedented quantities. After 600 the Scythians of South Russia began to receive gold from Transylvania and the Altai, and later furs from the Arctic forests. In satisfying the latter demand the half-savage tribes of the Kama and the Upper Volga were enabled to advance from a belated Stone Age to a Metal Age; in their settlements great accumulations of bones of small fur-bearing animals explain the source of their new wealth.

The variety and volume of imported materials from the ruins of Nineveh and Babylon are greater than ever before. About 700 B.C. the invention of coined money gave a fresh impetus to trade and a new archæological clue to its extent.

It was, however, the maritime peoples, the Phœnicians of Syria and of their colony, Carthage, and still more the Greeks, who took the fullest advantage of the new opportunities. Greek pottery—which, though beautifully hand-painted and highly esteemed to-day, is known to have been mass-produced in small factories—provides a good and durable index of such commerce. Excavation unearths surprising quantities of Greek vases, manufactured between 600 and 450 B.C. in Egypt, on the Gulf of Akaba, in Palestine, coastal Syria, and the Orontes valley, on the plateaux of Asia Minor, and all round the coasts of the Mediterranean and the Black Sea; they reach the Persian capital beyond the Tigris and furnish chieftains' graves on the Kuban, the middle Dnieper, and even the Marne. At the same time hoards of Greek coins are dispersed from Western Iran to Tunisia and Spain.

On the other hand, careful study discloses that good imitations of Athenian vases were being made in the cities of Italy and the Black Sea coast after 450 B.C. They are so good that one suspects that the colonial industries were at least started by experts from Athens. Old Greece exported not only manufactures, but also craftsmen, as European countries exported first manufactured goods and then machines for making them, naturally with engineers and operatives to instal and work them, during the nineteenth century.

In the sequel both processes were extended. For instance, archæologists happen to have studied the distribution of jars made in Rhodes between 300 and 200 and doubtless sent out full of wine or oil. They turn up in North Africa, all over Mesopotamia and Syria, round the Black Sea, in Italy and Sicily, and in barbarian villages on the Lower Danube. In the first centuries of our era trade circulated freely throughout the vast Roman Empire, whose boundaries are recognizable archæologically from the Firths of Clyde and Forth to the Sahara and Arabian Deserts and from the Atlantic to the Black Sea and the Euphrates. Pottery, made in Italy and duly stamped there, can be dug up in South Russia, Asia Minor, Palestine, Egypt, and Spain, and that of France in Sicily, North Africa, Egypt, and Britain. As luxuries these wares, together with glass vases, bronze casseroles, and coins, travelled far beyond the Empire's formidable frontiers to the Orkneys, Denmark, East Prussia, and Poland. In India, Ceylon, and even China, Roman coins are archæological reflexions of a trade in perishable substances—pepper, spices, silk—for which there is ample literary testimony.

After A.D. 450, with the disruption of the Roman Empire, trade naturally dwindled to small proportions in barbarized Europe. The succeeding centuries are really Dark Ages, because sites then inhabited so seldom yield imports from the still-civilized Mediterranean that would enable archæologists to date the occupation precisely. Of course intercourse did not cease, but has left few concrete traces in the archæological record. Only it may have been raiders rather than traders who brought Byzantine silver to the Lothians in the fourth century and to East Anglia in the sixth, and later left a trail of Persian and Arabic coins all across Russia to Scandinavia and Britain.

On the other hand, in Asia and Africa trade was very probably still expanding on the old lines. The archæological evidences might be illustrated by finds of Chinese porcelain in Islamic cities, or more graphically from inventories of the relics recovered from the buried cities of Central Asian deserts—in Turfan and the Tarim basin. But it lies outside the scope of this brief sketch to trace the growth of Oriental commerce and the revival of European trade to meet and eventually absorb it; for the archæological proofs can be enlivened by ample written texts. Both sources could be combined to show that the result of such intercourse was not only to enrich citizens' diets, but also to diffuse inventions. Windmills, porcelain, paper, and printing, all derived from Asia, would provide pertinent examples. But space will not permit.

We must, on the other hand, insist again that all this transportation of substances and commodities and the pooling of ideas that it reflects was conditioned by physical means of communication. We began in palæolithic times with scattered human groups separated by seas, mountains, swamps, and trackless forests. The fastest travel was on foot, the sole means of transport women's backs (judging by contemporary savages). Some upper palæolithic societies must have possessed boats of a sort; meso-lithic societies certainly did, since they settled on islands like Oransay and left paddles in Danish peat-mosses. North Europeans could by then transport burdens over snow on sledges the runners of which are preserved in mesolithic peats. Doubtless con-temporary steppe folk in Asia and North Africa possessed the same device.

The decisive advance achieved between 4000 and 3000 B.C. was to shift the loads from women's backs to asses' packs in North-eastern Africa, or to ox-drawn carts in Hither Asia, and to harness winds to assist rowers in propelling boats. Wagon and sailing-ship were conditioned by, but also conditions for, the use of metal. But the heavy vehicles of the third millen-nium, with solid wheels turning in one piece with the axle, were slow and lumbering. Travel was accelerated soon after 2000 B.C. by the invention of spoked wheels and the substitution of swift horses for asses or plodding oxen; though ancient horse-harness, consisting of the yoke, against which oxen had pushed with their broad shoulders, supplemented by a breast-band that pressed upon the horse's wind-pipe as he pulled, seriously reduced the efficiency of the new motive power. But the light horse-drawn chariot was used primarily as an engine of war, though it undoubtedly speeded up communications in the Near East. (The greater stability of Oriental empires of the second millennium, as compared with those of the third, has been attributed to the accelera-tion of official journeys by the use of chariots.)

Still, no wheeled vehicle would be much use in moun-tainous or wooded countries without roads, and the cost of road-building for more than a few miles was prohibitive without iron tools. Even in the early Iron Age, when an army crossed a stream the chariots had to be dismantled and swum across in pieces, as a lively Assyrian sculpture relates! You might get a cartload of grain a couple of miles to a village. A pack-ass could go almost anywhere, but an ass-load is small. Bulk transport in the Bronze Age was inevitably water-borne. Canals in the Tigris–Euphrates delta were roads as well as irrigation channels. Egyptian, Sumerian, and Indus cities could expand as they did just because foodstuffs from large areas could be carried by river and canal to feed the urban populations; Egyptian paintings show cattle and sheep in barges on the Nile. Water-borne traffic was, in fact, encouraged both by improvements in shipbuilding already mentioned and by the construction of harbours and ports in Hither Asia, Egypt, and Crete.

Early in the Iron Age camel-breeding opened a new era in desert transportation, and the development of equitation—riding as opposed to driving—accelerated intercourse. Bridge-building and road-building began in earnest. Foodstuffs could be gathered within a radius of 30 to 50 miles to support urban populations. Real cities in the Iron Age are no longer invariably located close to the sea or a navigable river.

Yet, the areas of Greek and Phœnician cities near the coast, rivalling or exceeding those of the riverine cities of the Bronze Age, may well imply dependence on sea-borne food supplies. At the same time the predominantly coastal distribution of goods exported for popular consumption as indexed by pottery (p. 66) would of itself justify the inference, confirmed by written testimony, that long-distance trade in cheap and bulky merchandise was still mainly conducted by sea.

The Roman roads that can still be traced were the most effectual attempt at relieving the disabilities of land-transport. They were, of course, primarily strategic, but, even so, had to carry heavy traffic like the supplies for the armies. And goods were certainly transported great distances far beyond the termini of all roads. But these were mainly luxuries, or became such by transport. Glass vases and bronze casseroles may have been cheap enough within the

Empire.   In Denmark they were appropriate furnishings for a chieftain's grave.

Roman roads and Roman harbours, too, were allowed to fall into disrepair in Europe's Dark Ages. Nevertheless the invention of the horse-collar—it is represented in European paintings about A.D. 900— did something to offset this loss; for at last the steed could exert his tractive power without choking himself on the breast-band imposed on him with the ox-yoke for at least 3,000 years.   However, it was the development of the sailing-ship (which gradually ousted the older galley) that opened up the supplies and the markets requisite for the Industrial Revolution.

The stages in this process have been described often enough.   It will suffice here to recall that the teapot, the tobacco pipe, and the enema symbolize the diffusion to, and absorption in, Atlantic civilization of discoveries and cultural traditions from China and the two Americas.   Rotary querns, wheel-made pots, and cowrie-shells are indicators of a like process 3,000 to 30,000 years earlier.   The range of the imports received by any society—i.e., any archæological " culture "—serves the prehistorian as a rough measure of the extent of the pool from which it might possibly draw traditions and to which it might possibly contribute.   In upper palæolithic times the maximum range would have been about 500 miles.   Till 4000 B.C. it was not very much wider, but by 2000 it had grown ten times.   A Mesopotamian city like Kish received imports from peninsular India, the Indus, Northern Afghanistan, Asia Minor, and the Mediterranean coasts about 2500 B.C.   But about A.D. 750 its successor, Baghdad, could draw materials from the whole of Eurasia and a large part of Africa. The pool had become almost continental.   By 1850 it had become global.   Unfortunately only a few emu's eggs will attest archæologically Australia's contribution, if the literary tradition be entirely erased by a few more global wars.

This chapter should logically be followed by one

on war. But though weapons and fortifications constitute a very prominent element in the archæologist's material, their study does not reveal any progressive regularities of the kind sought in this book. The continual improvement of weapons is, indeed, obvious enough, but the development of armour and defensive works is no less patent. So it is impossible to decide whether weapons have really become more effective, and war consequently more destructive. Nor is it clear whether wars have become more or less frequent. As to the object of wars, archæology of course affords no clues, while even history reveals that the results of wars are often the reverse of their proclaimed ends. We shall therefore limit ourselves to some brief hints as to the antiquity of warfare and its part in stimulating the exploitation of discoveries and inventions, and in their diffusion.

Individual animals often fight each other, and even whole packs are reported to engage in sanguinary conflicts. By middle palæolithic times, at least, men had specialized weapons, if only for hunting. But one man of that age, buried in a cave on Mt. Carmel, had been wounded with a sharp object—Keith thinks with a spear. Upper palæolithic, or perhaps only mesolithic, paintings on rocks in Eastern Spain depict combats between bowmen. A mesolithic man buried at Teviec, in Brittany, had been killed by arrows armed with microlithic flints, one of which was sticking in his backbone.

Some late neolithic villages were fortified. Stone mace-heads and perforated axes or flint daggers or lance-heads are found regularly in male barbarians' graves, particularly in Northern Europe during the later neolithic stage. They certainly look like weapons of war rather than of the chase. Thereafter metallurgy seems to have been first applied to the provision of reliable weapons (p. 34)—daggers and axes. Battle-scenes were depicted shortly before 3000 B.C., both in Mesopotamia (chiefly on seals) and in Egypt, where even a naval battle seems to be represented. After the Urban Revolution such themes became still more popular. Sumerian sculptures and mosaics portray an organized and disciplined army, consisting of light infantry, chariotry, and heavy infantry. The latter were protected with stout body-shields and copper helmets and fought in phalanx formation—tactics which historians had believed were invented by the Macedonians 2,000 years later. At the same time the Sumerian cities of the early third millennium were defended by deep ditches and brick walls. Even barbarian citadels of the same age, like Troy on the Dardanelles, were protected by strong stone ramparts.

In the sequel it was primarily as an engine of war that the chariot was lightened and accelerated after 2000 B.C. (p. 68). (It is worth noting incidentally that its use in war was abandoned by the Assyrians only after 700, by the Greeks after 600, by the continental Celts after 200, by the Britons of Southern England after 50 B.C., by those of Scotland after A.D. 80, and in Ireland later still!) During the same millennium daggers were elongated into rapiers 2 or 3 feet long (the earliest example comes from Crete about 1800) and were converted into cut-and-thrust swords apparently by barbarians in Europe shortly before 1200 B.C.

Iron was used first of all for tools. But, by making metal weapons cheap and accessible to all, it probably encouraged warfare at least among barbarians. One suspects that only barbarian chiefs and the soldiers equipped by civilized States could afford rapiers, helmets, and the rest of the costly bronze gear. In any case the multiplication of gigantic fortresses is an outstanding feature of the Iron Age in Europe. Stupendous though these works—of which formidable remains may still be seen on many an English and Scottish hill—appear by contrast with the flimsy hovels within them (the ramparts of masonry laced with timbers on Finavon Hill near Forfar were 20 feet thick and 12 to 16 feet high), they are entirely overshadowed by the defences erected by contemporary civilized societies. The walls of Babylon about 600 B.C. with a perimeter of 11 miles were over 86 feet thick, so that a pair of four-horse chariots could drive abreast along the rampart walk! The Great Wall of China, built about 200 B.C., 1,500 miles long and 15 to 30 feet high, is easily the largest alteration in the earth's surface effected by man till the twentieth century.

Still, offence kept pace with defence. Sapping was practised by the Assyrians, and among the Romans seems to have inspired the development of some of the ingenious tools mentioned on p. 39. Assyrian sculptures depict scaling-ladders, battering-rams, and wheeled towers before 650 B.C. After 400 the Greeks began to use artillery, " fired " of course by torsion, not explosives. At the same time cavalry, developed apparently by the steppe folk of Central Asia, accelerated the speed of attack enormously; even the Great Wall failed in the long run to keep the nomad horsemen out of China. It would be pointless to continue this recital by adducing figures of the size or cost of mediæval and later fortifications or of the new weapons that rendered them obsolete, or to enumerate the inventions like explosives, developed primarily for military ends, for which more humane uses have been found during brief intervals of truce.

Warfare has, however, contributed to progress not only as a stimulant to invention, but also as an agent in diffusion, being the concomitant or condition of invasion and conquest. Prehistorians can observe the replacement of one " culture " by another over wide areas of Europe and Hither Asia. Such changes in the archæological equivalent of barbarian societies are usually attributed to migrations replacing one society by another. In North and Central Europe, for instance, in the late neolithic stage, collective tombs and cemeteries of flat graves were replaced by individual burials under barrows furnished with weapons and ornaments different from those found in the earlier tombs and cemeteries, and with pots of novel form decorated in accord with new principles of composition.   Such changes are usually explained by postulating an invasion of " barrow-builders " who would at the same time have introduced fresh devices such as perforated axes and a more pastoral economy.   Again, at the beginning of the Late Bronze Age, burial of cremated bones encased in cinerary urns laid out in flat cemeteries termed urn-fields took the place of burials under barrows; with the change in ritual, cut-and-thrust swords began to take the place of stabbing-rapiers, new forms of orna-ment and the new craft tools mentioned on p. 35 appear.   This transformation, it is claimed, was due to a rather slow migration of " Urnfield-folk," who, starting most probably in South-eastern Germany, in time reached England, Spain, Upper Italy, the Balkans, the Western Ukraine, Poland, and Denmark (Germans, however, who are the most enthusiastic exponents of this theory, deny any invasion of North Germany or Denmark).   These would have spread not only the new rites, tools, and weapons, but also the techniques and distributive mechanism that cheapened bronze (p. 35).   On the other hand, it is admitted in each case that archæologically survivals of the former cultures can be detected in most areas. Hence the invaders would not have exterminated the conquered populations, but mingled with them or enslaved them.   The resultant cultures accordingly exhibit a blend of autochthonous adaptations to the local environment with adaptations evolved to meet the distinct conditions of the invaders' cradles.

Marxist prehistorians in Russia reject this migra-tionist explanation, claiming that changes in funerary ritual or ceramic decoration are merely ideological reflexions of changes in kinship organization and property relations brought about by technological advances.   So communal burial in collective tombs would correspond to an economy in which the basic means of production are owned communally by the clan, as they are among predominantly agricultural barbarians.   Individual interment under barrows, on the contrary, would be appropriate to more pastoral patriarchal societies, since cattle, now the chief form of wealth, are owned severally by patriarchal families; the grave-furniture would be more bellicose, because the new form of wealth, cattle, offers a more attractive prize for warring than crops or game.   In the sequel, families rich in cattle might become an aristocracy confirmed in their predominance by the exclusive ability to purchase costly bronze weapons. If the cheapening of such weapons in the Late Bronze Age undermined the aristocrats' military and social power, the urnfield could be presented as the symbol of a more equalitarian regime; it would then naturally appear, as it does, just where the new distributive mechanisms were established and the new technical processes applied.   Hence, instead of an " Urnfield migration " we should have a series of parallel social revolutions provoked by the technological advances and commercial reorganizations that are alone concretely demonstrated by the archæological finds.

A bourgeois prehistorian is predisposed by his training to under-estimate the Marxist arguments' cogency.   I shall frankly admit that their account fits many of the facts better than does the migrationist hypothesis.   The cradle of the " barrow-builders " is still undefined, that of the " Urnfield folk " disputable.   The several changes in burial pottery, ornaments, and weapons respectively are not so universally associated together as the foregoing compressed summary might suggest..   Nevertheless the evidence for prehistoric migrations is very much the same as that for historic migrations after A.D. 200 that are fully described by Greek and Roman authors. Moreover, at least in Britain, most skeletons buried in collective tombs are long-headed; those from the earlier individual graves are of a different round-head type that could hardly be evolved suddenly out of long heads by a social change alone.   Hence allowance should still be made for quite extensive movements of people among illiterate barbarians too. By introducing methods of farming, house-building, and heating appropriate to their original habitat and substances and plants native thereto, they could make useful contributions to the culture of the conquered territory, however much damage the conquest might at first involve.

If this be admitted in the case of Europe, then the changes in culture in the several levels of a tell in the Near East should be explained in the same way, even though the same site were continuously inhabited for centuries, as was seldom the case in Europe till the Middle Ages. In Thessaly, Asia Minor, Syria, Mesopotamia, and Iran at various levels in the settlement mounds, corresponding of course to periods in the villages' prehistory, complete changes are noticeable in pot-forms and decoration, in architecture and burial rites. But elements of continuity are even more prominent than in Europe—at Tepe Gawra, for example, the temples at every level are built on the same spot, though the plans may change. It is therefore still more doubtful than in Europe how far we should invoke conquests and immigrations—as opposed to internal social development and peaceful intercourse with neighbouring societies.

That the war-like conquests of civilized States acted as agents of diffusion is quite obvious from the archæological record. Soon after 2400 B.C. historical kings of Akkad (in Southern Mesopotamia) founded, in Assyria and on the Khabur in Syria, temples and palaces in which they left their inscriptions. Thereby villages of illiterate barbarians were converted into small outposts of the civilized urban economy. Such they remained in the sequel, though politically independent of Akkad and actually developing their own forms of civilization. In the Iron Age the colonies forcibly planted by the Phœnicians and Greeks on the barbarian shores of the Western Mediterranean are replicas of the true cities of the Eastern Mediterranean and, like them, centres of the urban economy. The conquests of Alexander the Great and his successors in Asia, right to the Oxus and the Indus, are marked by similar colonial cities of Greek form from which Greek art and Greek technology irradiated the native Asiatic populations so effectively that the results were visible in sculpture and painting, flour-milling and husbandry, long after Greek rulers had died out. Similarly, the Roman conquest brought Western Europe, including England, into a civilized economic system symbolized by cities of Mediterranean plan. Armies themselves might be agents of diffusion even where their advance was not followed by permanent conquest. The earliest rotary querns found in Scotland seem to be those from the Roman station at Newsteads, while those adopted by free natives in the unconquered north derive from what Dr. Curwen calls the legionary type.

One very concrete result of intercourse, peaceful and warlike, has been the expansion of civilization itself measured archæologically by the physical remains of cities. About 2500 B.C. such shone out like isolated stars or tiny clusters in the night of illiterate barbarism only on the Nile, the lower Tigris–Euphrates, and the Indus. A thousand years later cities form a continuous constellation from Egypt, Crete, and Central Turkey to the mountains of Western Iran, and one star is dawning on the Yellow River. Before 500 B.C. the constellation has become a galaxy embracing the whole Mediterranean basin, with the Black Sea coasts, Iran, India, and Southern Arabia with another nebular cluster in China. By A.D. 50 the western galaxy expands to the Irish and North Sea coasts and across the Alps to the Danube, while the Chinese cluster is spreading out to meet it in Central Asia. After 500 a single galaxy girdles Eurasia from the Pacific to the Atlantic, despite many dark patches and the waning of some bright stars in the west.

CHAPTER VI

FUNERALS

THE human activities so far considered are for the
most part directed to the satisfaction of obvious needs
which men share with other animals. The monuments and relics whose development has been traced
abstractly can all be regarded as helping to provide
food, shelter, and defence. In satisfying these aims
men behave with infinitely greater foresight than
any dumb brute. But the " ideas " underlying this
activity should be comprehensible to a rabbit or a
mouse. The difference in behaviour of *Homo sapiens*
and *Mus arvicola* seems to be one of degree. In
neither case has the scientific observer any serious
difficulty in deciding what his subject was getting at.
But archæologists can observe men doing things no
other animals have been found doing, behaving in a
distinctively human way—burying their dead fellows,
mutilating themselves, drawing pictures in dark, in-
accessible caverns, deliberately destroying food or
weapons by burning them or throwing them into
lakes. Such actions are presumably inspired by
wants and desires that other creatures do not experience. They are commonly and contradictorily labelled
material expressions of man's " spiritual culture."
We must now see whether any progressive changes
in that culture comparable to those so clearly revealed
in material culture can be observed in 50,000 years.

But first a word of warning. All the archæologist
can study is man's behaviour, the material expression
of his spiritual experiences. He cannot recapture
Neandertal man's ideas about " a future life " nor
the " theory " of Cro-Magnon magic. It may legitimately be questioned whether palæolithic men had
any spoken articulate language in which to express
in words " ideas " or " theories." Their language
may still have been kinetic—gestures and inarticulate

78

grunts capable of arousing in their fellows emotions
and spurring them to action, but not of formulating
an idea as abstract as even " bear." We must not
imagine men elaborating a theory of magic or a
theology and then acting on it. The deep emotions
aroused by the recurrent crises of life and death found
expression in no abstract words nor " judgments,"
but in concrete and passionate acts. The acts were
the ideas, not expressions of them. Certain sorts of
acts came to be recognized by society as appropriate
in certain situations, just as certain types of tool were
approved by tradition as standard forms. Such
patterns of behaviour became rites. But the rite did
not necessarily express a theory; more probably it
constituted it. Only after thousands of human
generations did individuals, themselves generally
withdrawn from the more urgent preoccupations of
life, and often schooled in abstract thinking by writing, even begin to explain or justify the rites in
analytical language. With these, archæologists are
not concerned. In the beginning was the deed, and
that is all archæology can hope to grasp.

Of deeds of this sort the record of burials is the
longest and most complete—though far from complete, since the lying-in-state, the cortège, the wake,
the games, and other accessories of funerals attested
in literature have left but small impression on the
archæological record.

Even the sub-human Neandertalers who hunted
mammoths in Europe some 50,000 years ago were
at pains to inter ceremonially their deceased children
and kinsmen. They dug a pit in the floor of the
cave they inhabited and buried the body in a ritual
position—flexed or contracted. With it they placed
joints of game, flint knives and hand-axes, and lumps
of ochre—food, weapons, and toilet articles. In one
grave at La Ferrassie (Dordogne) the body was
partly covered and protected by a stone slab, the under-
side of which was embellished with small hollows
artificially hammered out—what are called cup-marks.

In upper palæolithic times the ritual was more varied and the grave-furniture richer. Some bodies lie extended at full length, others flexed, others again crouched with the knees drawn up to the chin; both extended and contracted burials were represented, though at different levels, in the Grimaldi caves near Mentone. One grave contained the bodies of a woman and two children. In several graves the bones are stained with red ochre, as if the corpse had been thickly sprinkled with or embedded in the red colouring-matter. The dead may be decked with necklaces, chaplets, or anklets of perforated shells—sometimes, in the Dordogne, cowrie-shells brought all the way from the Mediterranean—and pendants or bracelets of mammoth ivory.

Finally, the mesolithic phase introduces further variations. Not all the burials of this period come from caves; some are found in encampments in the open, generally in the refuse of the camp. At Offnet, in Bavaria, thirty-three skulls, detached from their trunks, but all covered with red ochre, had been buried together in a cave. In a Crimean cave a male and female skeleton lay extended side by side. And in the cave of El Wad, Mount Carmel, some Natufians (p. 17) were buried extended in groups of five or six, while others were interred individually in the flexed attitude. It would be pointless to catalogue the curiosities of funerary ritual observable in later phases of social development. If, however, we confine our attention to widespread practices, and consider each aspect of burial separately, some general progressive tendencies can be recognized.

It would be tempting, though probably illegitimate, to regard the practice of sprinkling the corpse with red ochre as a mistaken attempt to bring back life by restoring to the palid corpse the colour of life. If so, men took a long time to recognize the futility of the practice, for it was observed among the neolithic hunters of the North European forest zone, among neolithic cultivators in the Danube and Rhine valleys, in Iran (at Sialk I–II), and even in China. It lingered on into the early Bronze Age in Spain and Italy, and longest of all in South Russia, but died out among all civilized peoples.

Extended burial was the rule among neolithic hunters in the Siberian and North European forest zones and among some neolithic farming communities in France, Northern Europe, and South Russia, and in the al'Ubaid phase in Syria and Mesopotamia. But the normal practice of neolithic and Early Bronze Age societies was burial in a flexed or contracted posture. It subsequently began to give place to extended burial. In Egypt, first nobles and then other classes adopted this posture. In one cemetery already by the Pyramid Age (Dynasty IV), only 40 per cent of the corpses were contracted; six centuries later only the very poorest, 4 per cent of the total, were so treated. An equally gradual change is observable in Greece between 1600 and 1400 B.C. as society grew richer, and similarly in Sicily a couple of centuries later. In the Iron Age contracted burial persisted in only a few enclaves in the British Isles, North-eastern Italy, Transylvania, Transcaucasia, and the Iranian mountains; in Scotland it lasted till A.D. 200!

The evidence from Egypt, Greece, and Sicily precludes the notion that extended burial was a distinctively Nordic rite, as exclusive attention to Continental Europe would at first sight suggest. Extended burial is fairly definitely associated with increasing wealth and superior tools that meant, among other things, warmer bedding and facilities for digging larger graves. There is no evidence that the abandonment of contracted burial was due to a change of race, nor yet of belief.

Meanwhile a third method of disposal of the dead—cremation—had enjoyed a wide vogue, at least in Europe. Practised already by neolithic societies in the British Isles, Brittany, Switzerland, and Central Germany, and perhaps also in Greece, Syria, and Palestine, cremation became the favourite burial method in Britain and Northern and Central Europe in the Middle–Late Bronze Age (from 1400 B.C.), and in Spain and Upper Italy, too, by the Early Iron Age (from 1000 B.C.); it was practised also at Troy on the Dardanelles, Carchemish on the Euphrates, and occasionally in Crete and Greece, between 1400 and 1000 B.C. In the first millennium B.C. both cremation and inhumation were practised in most Greek and Italic cities; the Celts in Western Europe generally inhumed, while the Teutons in the north still cremated. Since the earliest Phœnician (Semitic) colonists at Motya in Sicily practised only cremation, it cannot be regarded as an " Aryan " rite. But it was never popular in Asia (except in India), and even at Motya the later Phœnician burials are inhumations. In the Roman Empire cremation at first spread without ousting inhumation, but at the same time some Teutonic tribes were reverting to inhumation. After A.D. 200 the popularity of cremation was waning even in the European provinces of the Empire before its conversion to Christianity, but it remained the favourite rite among Slavonic peoples and the Scandinavian Teutons till their conversion.

Cremation graves are on the whole no less richly furnished than inhumations; for example, the richest Bronze Age graves in Britain contain cremated bones, and so do the richest graves in the Early Iron Age cemetery of Hallstatt in Austria. That hardly agrees with the popular notion that cremation, involving the annihilation of the physical remains of the departed, was inspired by a more spiritual conception of the soul. Nor can the rite be connected exclusively with any particular race or people, even in India, Greece, and Italy. In any case, cremation never ousted inhumation. Christianity adopted the rite practised in contemporary Palestine and reviving in the Roman Empire when the new creed spread there.

The converse practice of conserving as completely as possible the physical remains of the defunct reached its logical development in Egypt. There the hot desert sand in which prehistoric corpses had been buried acted as a preservative, so that hair and flesh are still intact on bodies we dig up after 5,000 or 6,000 years. With growing wealth, however, the bodies were encased in stone sarcophagi or clay or wooden coffins, presumably to preserve them even better. The result was, of course, the reverse, since, removed from contact with the disinfecting sand, the soft parts quickly succumbed to putrefaction. To avoid this, mummification was gradually developed after 2500 B.C., first for the Pharaoh and his nobles, later for all who could afford the fees. The costly and complicated process carried out by a guild of professional embalmers with their own specialized craft tools was in practice confined to Egypt, though curiously similar preservative methods were employed by some barbarian tribes as far away as South America and the Pacific. But clay coffins were adopted in Mesopotamia by 2300 B.C. and in Crete by 1800. And stone sarcophagi were carved for the kings of Byblos as early as 1800 B.C. and used later by Assyrian kings, all well-to-do Phœnicians both in Syria and in their colonies in North Africa, Sicily, and Spain, and so by similar classes among Greeks, Etruscans, Romans, and other ancient peoples. From these the Christians learnt the idea that they have subsequently preserved.

Our palæolithic forerunners had deposited with the departed food, ornaments, toilet articles, and weapons. In general, neolithic and later societies followed this hoary precedent. But of course with technical progress the gear men used and wore multiplied enormously. On the whole, neolithic and Early Bronze Age graves reflect this advance. They may be furnished with numerous pots, presumably containing food and drink, and perhaps unguents or paints; combs, palettes, and other toilet articles; in the Bronze Age also with mirrors, tweezers, and razors; with imported shells and hard stone beads, later pins, anklets, neckrings, and earrings of metal; and finally with weapons—stone axes, flint arrow-heads, daggers, and knives or the metal versions thereof.

But certain items added to human equipment since the Old Stone Age are mysteriously absent. Though agriculture had revolutionized human life, agricultural implements are hardly ever found in graves at any time. I know no neolithic graves containing sickles, and in the Bronze Age only seven or eight in Central Europe and one in South Russia. Querns have been reported from about half a dozen neolithic graves (in Cyprus and Central Europe), but from none of the Bronze or Iron Ages anywhere (before A.D. 200).

Secondly, the only tool regularly found in graves of all periods is the knife. Axes are, indeed, common enough, but they might be, and often demonstrably were, weapons. Craft tools are very exceptionally found in graves. Unambiguous carpenter's tools of stone, like gouges, are known from one small group of Swedish graves and a few tombs in Southern Spain. The more specialized metal tools, like saws, are represented only in two very early Spanish graves, in several Sumerian graves, but all before 2400 B.C., and in Egyptian graves of like antiquity. Smith's tools, like moulds, are even rarer. The highly specialized and diversified craft equipment of Iron Age craftsmen is entirely unrepresented in the sepulchral record. It seems, therefore, fair to infer that the instruments of production by means of which human societies since palæolithic times have been extending their control over nature were not normally buried with their users.

(Two reservations must be made. Among the Teutons of the Dark Ages from A.D. 400 to 800 blacksmith's tools and agricultural implements like scythes may be found even in warriors' graves. Egyptian tombs, especially between 2000 and 1750 B.C., often contain model craft tools or pictures of such. But as these tombs belong to nobles, and even ladies, the instruments were clearly intended for use not by the tomb's owner, but by his or her " ghost servants.")

After the Early Bronze Age, in certain provinces
and among certain societies the grave furniture not
only fails to keep pace with society's growing wealth,
but actually becomes poorer and more exiguous.
For instance, in Britain, while axes, rapiers, swords,
spears, and even shields and cauldrons of the Middle
and Late Bronze Age, are found in numbers, stray or
in hoards, none of these weapons or utensils has ever
been found in graves, the furniture of which is reduced
to an occasional bone pin, bead, or bronze razor.
Just the same impoverishment of grave-goods has
been noted in the later interments in Sicily and South
Russia, where Bronze Age societies developed without interruption for some fifteen centuries. It is only
slightly less obvious in Denmark, where the earlier
Bronze Age graves are very richly furnished with
costly metal weapons and ornaments which were later
replaced by miniatures or omitted. The same tendency reasserted itself between A.D. 200 and 400 after
luxurious grave furniture had become again the rule
during the earlier years of our era, when commerce
with the Roman Empire first affected Danish society
directly.

The sepulchral record of civilized societies tells the
same tale. For instance, only the earlier burials in
Assyrian cemeteries are well furnished with bronze
weapons and ornaments. After 2000 B.C., though
the cities were far richer and the houses larger, the
graves contain as a rule only a few token ornaments
and vases. In Egypt an inclination to replace valuable possessions, like oxen or finely worked flint
knives, by cheap models in wood or clay is perceptible even in predynastic graves. It culminated
early in the second millennium when a rich landowner
took with him to the grave his farm and barn replete
with agricultural instruments, livestock, and per-
sonnel, his boat with its crew, a host of personal
attendants, and even a bodyguard fully armed; but
all in the shape of the lively clay models, examples of
which you will now find in most museums.

In the Classical world the citizens of the still poor
Greek States of the Dark Age, before 700 B.C., might
be buried with their arms and jewellery. In later
cemeteries, both in old Greece and in her colonies in
Sicily and Italy, the grave-goods are poorer, though
the cities were now rich; the furniture normally consists of vases, lamps, and figurines of clay, all beautiful, but actually factory-made and very cheap, less
often of mirrors, strigils, gamesmen, and ornaments
of very thin gold, made apparently for funerary use,
exceptionally a horse or a dog or a fine metal vase—
in any case a tiny fraction of the deceased's possessions.
Wealth as such was not left in the tomb. In particular, abstract wealth—money, whether coined or
in the form of the spits (*obols*) that preceded coins in
Greece and Italy—is represented in graves only
symbolically by a single " penny " (save, funnily
enough, among the Semitic Carthaginians, in whose
tombs coins may be more numerous).

The foregoing principles do not at first sight seem
to apply to all territories or periods. The cemeteries
of many barbarian tribes in Europe during the Bronze
Age, and still more in the Iron Age, and that even in
the Christian era, often yield the excavator a treasure
of costly weapons, vases, ornaments, and horse-trap-
pings with imported luxury articles. Barbarian
cemeteries in Transcaucasia, the Iranian mountains,
and Central Asia are sometimes equally rich. But
everywhere the cemeteries in question seem to cover
at most two or three centuries; most belong to
tribes that have established themselves in a region
for a time and then are either replaced by other
tribes with a quite different equipment and " culture "
or come into such close contact with more highly
civilized societies—Greek, Etruscan, Roman, Babylonian, Byzantine, Chinese—that their barbarian
social organization is disrupted, as we see happening
to-day where European civilization impinges too
abruptly on " primitive " tribes. So the cemeteries
in question do not belong to stable societies de-

veloping autonomously for a really substantial period.

Again, there is no very obviously regular reduction in funerary furniture in Greece between 3000 and 1200 B.C. But the continuity of culture there was interrupted so radically about the end of the Early Bronze Age in 1800 B.C. as to imply a complete change of society—not merely the replacement of one dynasty or ruling group by another, as happened frequently in Babylonia without upsetting our rule. Of course, a still more violent interruption ended the Bronze Age about 1100. Moreover, between 1550 and 1400 B.C. Greece had been exposed to intense radiation from the advanced and luxurious Minoan civilization of Crete, as a flood of Minoan imports shows. Similarly in the township of Hissar, in Iran, though the site was occupied for 1,000 or 1,500 years without exhibiting any appreciable reduction in its grave-furniture, the continuity of culture was interrupted at two points, so that we are dealing with three societies rather than one.

The facts adduced, then, justify the following generalization: In a stable progressive society the tendency is for the grave-goods to diminish absolutely, or at least relatively; in other words, a diminishing proportion of society's growing wealth is buried with the dead. Perhaps this might be expressed thus: as possessions came to be regarded as commodities, as wealth, they were ever more grudgingly left with their former owners or users. There is no need to suppose that this process has been inspired by any change in ideas about the conditions of the dead. On the contrary, we know some of the reasons that accelerated it. A king of Sidon in Syria wrote on his sarcophagus: " Do not open the coffin-lid nor disturb me. No gold, no silver, no treasures lie in this box but (only) I." Greek cities and the Roman republic legislated to prohibit extravagance at funerals and forbade the deposition of gold or complete vases in graves. On the other hand, in early Christian

graves vases and lamps were still buried with the dead
in many cities (for instance, at Thebes, in Greece),
and even arms among recently converted barbarians
like the Franks. Subsequent legislation against such
" pagan " practices, whatever its phraseology, merely
followed Greco-Roman precedents.

At the same time the reduction of material offerings
cannot be regarded as a sign of declining affection
between kinsmen, nor of social disapproval of such
affection. (The very laws that restrict funerary
extravagance impose on the relatives the duty of
ensuring the decent burial of the deceased.) Hence
the new practices must have been in time justified
and confirmed by an appropriate ideology—less
material, more spiritual conceptions of the soul and
its future life.

We could in the same way trace a decline in the
tendance of the dead. The practice of making
periodical offerings at the tomb is attested archæologically in Egypt from 3000 B.C. and in Assyria from
2100, and throughout Greco-Roman civilization from
the Dark Age of Greece into Christian times. Whole
classes of Christian tombstones are to-day just copies
of the altars and receptacles for funerary offerings
standardized by Greek and Roman society. Indeed,
the periodical deposition of flowers on the grave, still
current even in Protestant countries, is just a survival
of the ancient practice of tendance of the dead reduced
to a purely symbolical form and spiritualized.

A consideration of the burial-place, the tomb itself,
will lead to very similar conclusions. The Neandertalers and upper palæolithic peoples had been buried
in caves. But as they had lived in the same caves,
we might equally well say that they were buried in
their dwellings. In fact, burial under house-floors
persisted into neolithic times, and even later among
some societies—the hunters of the North European
forests, some cultivators in Western Europe and
Southern Italy, the villagers of Merimde in Egypt and
Sialk in Iran, and later still in Spain and Hither

Asia—in fact, even in great cities in Mesopotamia and Syria. Beneath each better-class Assyrian or Babylonian house, even in the days of Nebuchadnezzar and later, was a convenient vault where the householder might rest with his fathers. The burial-chambers were by no means hermetically sealed, but the ancestral effluvium did not offend pious Assyrian nostrils. But most communities in neolithic and later stages preferred to bury their dead outside the inhabited area, in cemeteries or chamber tombs.

As an alternative to house-burial many neolithic societies round the Mediterranean used natural caves as burial-places, as had the Neandertalers 40,000 years before, but generally as communal ossuaries—a practice that persisted in South France right into the Early Iron Age. Some societies in the third millennium at least used to enlarge small natural grottos or cut artificial ones in chalk or soft stone to serve as communal ossuaries entirely with stone tools in Sicily, Southern Italy, Malta, Sardinia, Portugal, and along the Marne in France, aided perhaps by copper chisels in Syria, Cyprus, Greece, and South Russia. In any case the excavation of these rock-cut tombs with the simple equipment then available must have absorbed a great deal of social labour, and sometimes even more than was required to provide adequate accommodation for clansmen's skeletons.

For while many rock-cut tombs are small or irregular like natural caves, others have been carefully planned as if to reproduce underground the likeness of the round hut or rectangular house inhabited by the living. In Cyprus, Sicily, and Sardinia this likeness is enhanced by laborious carving of the rock in imitation of wooden door-posts and lintels. But at first these Mediterranean rock-cut tombs must, like the natural caves, have served as communal ossuaries, since they often contain the bones of hundreds of persons, generally in great disorder. But in Egypt, from 2750 B.C., chambers excavated in the hard rock, of course with copper chisels, normally contain only

a single body. Yet a noble's tomb thus quarried out
in hard granite was a subterranean replica of his
palace with many rooms, a distinct harem quarter, a
porter's lodge and even latrines. Such a rock-cut
house remained the standard tomb in Egypt in the
sequel. But in the second millennium the tomb did not
grow larger or more complicated, though the enormous increase of wealth was very adequately reflected
in the increased scale and luxury of domestic architecture.

In Sicily and the East Mediterranean, too, after
2000 B.C. the rock-cut tombs normally contain at
most only a score of corpses, and generally less. The
communal ossuary has turned into a family vault
used for three or four generations by members of a
group of close kinsfolk. A rectangular plan and
more imitative carving reflect improvements in house
construction, but not the growth in living space or
comfort of real dwellings. Then, with the help of
iron tools, the Etruscans in Italy, some peoples in
South-western Asia Minor, and the Medes in Iran
had the rafters, beams, and posts of their wooden
houses realistically reproduced in their sepulchral
chambers underground. From the Mediterranean
Iron Age the rock-cut tomb has passed into the
funerary tradition of Christendom, Jewry, and Islam.
One point is worth remembering. The finer rock-cut
ossuaries of the Marne or of Sardinia were more
substantial, and cost infinitely more labour to construct, than the flimsy hovels inhabited by their barbarian builders; the first Egyptian rock-cut tombs
were almost as spacious and commodious as, and far
more permanent than, their occupants' former palaces.
But the burial chambers excavated by the civilized
peoples of the Iron Age—let alone ourselves—cannot
compare in size, magnificence, or cost with the commodious urban mansions known from Olynthus,
Pompeii, and other Hellenistic, Roman, or Phœnician
towns.

To serve as communal ossuaries in parts of Crete,

Sicily, Sardinia, the Balearic Islands, Spain and Portugal, during the third millennium, but apparently only where hard rock made quarrying difficult, barbarian communities constructed above-ground stone chambers similar in form to the rock-cut tombs, and put them underground artificially by covering them with a cairn of stones or an earthen tumulus. Similar chambers were constructed also in areas where natural or artificial caves had never been used as ossuaries; sometimes, indeed, where such were available or could quite easily be excavated, notably in Brittany, the British Isles, and Northern Europe, by communities still possessed only of a neolithic equipment and no metal tools. They are often built of huge stones, and are therefore called megalithic (from the Greek *megas*, great, and *lithos*, stone).

The construction of a megalithic tomb with the equipment available in the third millennium was a stupendous feat. The chamber at Bagneux, Northwestern France, for instance, is 61 feet long, 16 feet wide and 9 feet high inside and composed of thirteen huge slabs. The largest of the roofing slabs measured 23 feet square, and must weigh 86 tons. Yet it had to be raised to the top of stone uprights, 9 feet above the ground, and that without the aid of any block and tackle. In Scotland, to cover their funerary chambers on the barren moors of Caithness, neolithic groups piled cairns 240 feet long that must contain some 135,000 cubic feet or 8,000 tons of stone— enough to build five parish churches! Yet their dwellings were certainly no better than those of Skara Brae described on p. 46.

Among better-equipped societies of later date funerary architecture never absorbed anything like this proportion of the resources available, save perhaps for some royal tombs described below. But megalithic tombs of modest dimensions were erected to serve as family vaults round the Caucasus in the later Bronze Age, and during the Iron Age the Etruscans and others built above ground reproduc-

tions of rock-cut house-tombs where geological
conditions prevented the excavation of such underground. Hence the mausoleum has passed into
modern cemeteries. The pretentious tombs with
house-fronts that were still erected in cemeteries last
century evidently embody an idea 5,000, nay 50,000,
years old. But whereas the long cairns and rock-cut
tombs prepared for the neolithic dead are more substantial and spacious than live barbarians' huts, their
recent descendants cannot vie in size nor elegance
with the commodious Victorian mansions whose
façades and doors the mason so diligently copied.

The progressive tendency disclosed by a study of
funerary architecture is that with the advance of
civilization more care is devoted to the comfort and
hygiene of dwelling-houses and less to the stability
of tombs. But once more that need not mean any
diminution of affection, and may be accompanied
by a spiritualization of the conception of the dear
departed's fate.

An apparent exception to the foregoing generaliza-
tions is constituted by a peculiar group of burials,
belonging to the Bronze Age or later archæological
periods, that may conveniently be termed Royal
Tombs. Closer inspection will show that they really
confirm our inferences. The class includes in the
Bronze Age the tombs of the earliest Egyptian
Pharaohs, the early dynastic royal tombs of Ur,
Kish, and Mari, those of Kerma in Nubia about
1800 B.C., the tombs of the Shangs, the first historical
kings of China at Anyang, the Shaft Graves of Mycenæ
and the later Tholos tombs; and in the Iron Age the
sixth-century Scythian barrows, the ship-burial of an
early Saxon king at Sutton Hoo, the ship-burials of
the Viking age in Norway, and some burials of Mongol
chiefs in Central Asia of still later date. All are
instructive as well as exciting, but only three can be
examined here.

The predynastic Egyptians, down to 3000 B.C., had
all been buried in a simple pit surmounted with a flimsy

superstructure of mudbrick to serve as a chapel of
offerings. Two tombs, both attributed to Menes
(Hor-Aha), the first Pharaoh to unite Upper Egypt
and the Delta under a single sovereignty, are sharply
contrasted with all earlier and contemporary com-
moners' graves. At Saqqara, near Cairo, his new
capital, Menes had built for him a huge " mastaba,"
a mud-brick superstructure 135 feet long by 50 feet
wide with whitewashed walls 8 feet thick and decorated
outside with alternating buttresses and recesses, and
enclosing twenty-seven magazine-chambers, beneath
which was dug the actual grave—a shaft 64 feet long
by 9 feet wide by 4 feet deep, roofed with planks and
beams of imported timbers. The remains left by
early plunderers show that the chambers had been
crammed with jars of wheat and wine and oil and
costly vases of hard stone.

His second tomb at the old capital of Abydos, in
Upper Egypt, was a shaft 39 feet by 31 feet, lined with
brick and timbers, near which were thirty-three small
tombs in a row, containing the bodies of the lesser
harem and of officials, while the tomb itself contained
remains of human victims who had undoubtedly been
slain to accompany their master. The surviving
furniture, comprising fragments of gold, silver, and
copper ornaments, weapons, vessels, and toilet
articles, and a conspicuous variety of imported
Asiatic materials and objects, gives one the impression
that a substantial proportion of the Pharaoh's wealth
was buried with him. The tombs are symbolic of the
political unification of Egypt and the creation of a
civilized State out of a collection of barbarian communities presumably organized on a kinship basis.
The Asiatic objects from the tombs and contemporary
sites, the temporary adoption of Asiatic devices and
artistic motives, bespeak an Asiatic element which
must be accommodated in the new society Menes
was helping to create.

In the sequel the tombs of later Pharaohs of dyn-
asties I and II grow larger and richer, save that

eventually the immolation of real concubines, officials, and servants was abandoned. But nobles and high officials, too, began to build them mastaba tombs, so that the distinction between king and noble was being lost. To reassert the uniqueness of kingship, Zoser of Dynasty III hit on the idea of piling five stone mastabas, of diminishing sizes, one on the top of the other, thus creating the first or Step Pyramid. It was 196 feet high and measured 410 by 357 feet along the base. It was set in a sacred enclosure 596 yards long by 306 yards wide; the stone walls of which, 32 feet high, were adorned with fluted pilasters that seem to anticipate the classical Grecian column. Next Cheops (Khufu) of Dynasty IV built the Great Pyramid, no less than 480 feet high and 755 feet square at the base, and containing some 2,300,000 blocks of stone with an average weight of $2\frac{1}{2}$ tons each. The blocks had to be quarried on the opposite bank of the Nile, floated across, and then dragged up a specially constructed ramp on to the plateau, and that without the aid of any pulleys or windlasses!

After Dynasty IV no more tombs were built on this scale. Kings, indeed, had pyramids, but modest in size and built of brick. Their bodies were preserved in rock-cut tombs not different in kind from those hewn for nobles as early as Dynasty III. Indeed, the tombs of the XVIIIth-dynasty kings were less complicated and hardly larger than those of the Old Kingdom nobles, though these kings, drawing tribute and plunder from an Asiatic Empire, were far richer than Menes or Zoser, and though even private houses were now more spacious than their tombs. Their burial-furniture was extravagantly rich, as the intact tomb of Tutankhamen has strikingly shown; but considering his revenues, one feels that only a small fraction of the royal wealth was buried with its owner.

So in Egypt royal tombs, distinguished qualitatively from all private graves by the magnitude of their architecture, by the inclusion of human victims, and by the large proportion of their owner's wealth buried within them, seem distinctive of an early stage in social development, when Egypt was emerging from tribal barbarism to civilization and exposed to strong foreign, Asiatic, influences.

The tombs of the earliest city-kings in Mesopotamia (if they are correctly diagnosed as royal tombs) in the third millennium, and of the first historical Chinese monarchs in the second, exhibit the same peculiarities—the exceptional size and architecture of the tombs, the wealth of grave-goods, the inclusion of livestock (asses, oxen, or elephants), and of human victims. And in each case we are witnessing the birth of a new civilization. In other cases an older civilization acts as midwife to barbarism in its travail.

In the Late Bronze Age the pastoral tribes of the Eurasiatic steppes buried their dead under barrows in pits or lean-to wooden shacks. After 700 B.C. the societies living between the Black Sea and the Caspian were exposed to the radiation of urban civilization through traders from the Greek colonies and Iranian kingdoms, and now found new sources of wealth in war and plunder. The royal barrows of the sixth century, on the Kuban, cover great wooden chambers crammed with ornate weapons, vessels, and ornaments of precious metals, and vases and luxury objects of Greek manufacture, and surrounded with hecatombs of horses and the skeletons of slaves. The barrow at Ulski aul was no less than 49 feet high, and covered the wooden frame of a rectangular tent set up on virgin soil, 24 feet long and 19 feet wide. Around it were the skeletons of 180 horses tethered to posts, while remains of fifty more horses were found in the barrow above it. In the fifth century the Scyths were richer and more civilized. Their kings reposed in handsome chamber-tombs that are, however, no longer so exceptional; they are still well furnished with precious metals, but by no means proportionately richer than the older barrows. The horse hecatombs have been reduced to two or four beasts, the slaves proportionately.

The Celtic chieftains' graves in Würtemberg and on the Marne, the ship-burial prepared for an East Anglian king at Sutton Hoo, and the burial of a Viking queen in the Oseberg ship,[1] all belong to a similar sociological phase—to barbarian societies suddenly irradiated from a much higher civilization: from the Etruscans and the Greek colony of Marseilles, from the surviving sparks of provincial Roman civilization and the young Frankish State, from Byzantium and the Merovingian Empire. In the last two cases States will arise. But the State may be still-born. There are no successors to the Nubian kings buried with human victims in great barrows at Kerma, nor to the Early Bronze Age chieftains on the Saale. Royal tholos tombs containing lavish treasures, imports from Minoan Crete, and the bones of slaves, cease in Greece with the Iron Age. But their backgrounds are quite similar.

Archæologists have found the tombs of other kings—of Byblos and Sidon in Phœnicia, Assyrian, Persian, and Roman Emperors. None differs in kind from contemporary graves; though admittedly larger and more ornate than these, they are insignificant in comparison with the palaces of the Assyrians or of Darius of Persia, or even the baths and other public buildings erected by the Roman Emperors. The mausoleum of Hadrian (built about A.D. 125), for example, consisted of a rectangular platform, 247 feet square, cased in white marble, on which rose a conical tumulus, the marble-faced plinth of which had a circumference of 1,000 feet. But this imposing monument was designed as a family vault, in which the ashes of his successors, too, were to be interred, just as earlier Cæsars from Augustus to Nerva reposed in the slightly smaller mausoleum built by the first.

---

[1] At Oseberg Queen Aasa lay in a genuine sea-going ship, 70 feet long with all its gear, two tents, four wagons, four sledges, four beds, thirteen horses, six dogs, a complete ox, chests, buckets, weaving utensils, craft tools, a complete kitchen outfit replete with a rotary quern and a handmaid to work it.

Yet the domains and revenues of a Cæsar exceeded more than a hundredfold that of any Pharaoh; a single imperial summer palace (at Splt) measured superficially 590 by 196 feet.

The significant fact is that all the monarchs just considered had inherited a firmly established State organization and based their dominions on long-civilized societies. Royal tombs of the extravagant type previously considered are confined to a single transitional stage in social evolution. Once that stage is passed, burials of royalties are amenable to the same generalization as had been induced from a study of commoner interments.

With the advance of civilization funeral rites and mortuary constructions have absorbed a diminishing proportion of social energy and resources. In the latest stages of barbarism and early civilization, among some societies at least, the construction of tombs and preparations for burial ceremonies seem to have been the principal object of the accumulation and expenditure of individual wealth. To-day the funeral is a major item in the life-budget only among the worst-paid class of Irish labourers or Polish peasants. That, however, does not of course mean any diminution of parental or filial affection. Were that measurable by archæology, it would doubtless prove to have increased, and the more economical means of its expression might appear to be correlated with a loftier ideology.

CHAPTER VII

SACRIFICE AND TEMPLE-BUILDING

THE uniquely human practice of destroying deliberately, and indeed ceremonially, food and other forms
of wealth is not so easily detectable by archæological
means as ritual burial, and its interpretation in logical
formulæ is inevitably still more hazardous. Nevertheless, a respectable pedigree can be established for
offerings or sacrifices.

Even the middle palæolithic occupants of certain
caves in the Swiss Alps and the Frankish Jura had
built against the cave walls altar-like enclosures of
stones in which had been carefully deposited the skulls
of cave-bears, their chief prey. The excavators and
some commentators like Menghin have interpreted
these deposits as offerings, citing the ceremonies of
bear-hunters in Eastern Siberia before the Soviet
revolution.

In upper palæolithic times very definite evidence
is forthcoming. Towards the close of the last ice
age a band of reindeer-hunters were wont to camp
every summer beside a little swampy lake near Ham-
burg. Bones and other refuse from their seasonal
encampment were thrown into this lake, where they
have been well preserved. Among them are complete
skeletons of reindeer weighted with a stone to ensure
their sinking. These trophies of the chase have therefore been destroyed, not eaten. We may say that
they have been " offered " or " sacrificed," and may
guess they represent the first-fruits of each season's
hunting. That would accord with the practice of
many savage tribes to-day.

Comparable offerings by neolithic farmers of grain
or meat are naturally much harder to recognize
archæologically. The practice must be inferred from
ethnographic evidence. Direct testimony to sacrifices of this kind is not forthcoming till 3000 B.C.,

98

and even thereafter the literary evidence is much fuller and more conclusive than the archæological. But other sorts of goods besides food are " sacrificed " by contemporary pagan societies, and of such offerings, too, archæology provides very early hints.

Travellers have recorded that aboriginal tribes in South America on occasions chop off a joint or two from fingers or thumbs as " offerings " to some deity, spirit, or magic power. Now in the dark recesses of the cave of Gargas in the Pyrenees human hands have been outlined. The silhouettes have indubitably been executed by early upper palæolithic reindeer hunters of the Gravettian or Aurignacian group. But all the hands are mutilated, as if some joints were missing from the digits. It really looks as if the paintings commemorate a sacrifice in the ice age of parts of the body of the kind approved by our South American savages. In fact, the actual bones of a woman buried with a man in mesolithic times in the cave of Murzhak-koba in the Crimea prove that some of her finger-joints had been deliberately amputated.

Among upper palæolithic societies in North Africa it was the practice to remove forcibly one or two incisor teeth, but whether the extraction was performed as a " sacrifice " of some kind or just in obedience to a tribal fashion, as among some Africans to-day, is naturally undiscoverable. Among progressive societies in the neolithic and later stages such bodily mutilations are rarely detectable. Those that are represented in the archæological record, such as circumcision among the Egyptians and skull-deformation in Cyprus and South Russia, are not necessarily to be explained as sacrifices.

Offerings of new forms of wealth for which the progress of civilization won social recognition are still less easily detected without the aid of written sources, save in connexion with tombs and temples. Nevertheless, accumulations of valuable weapons, ornaments, and utensils deposited in North European bogs during the Bronze and Iron Ages and as late as A.D. 700 are usually termed " votive " by Danish archæologists who regard them as sacrifices of a sort. They include gold vases, too thin for practical use, and even gold models of boats and other objects, so that the theory seems plausible.

The construction of sanctuaries and temples is itself a kind of sacrifice involving the consumption of valuable materials and labour. But such edifices seem to imply some notion of gods or deities more definite and concrete than can legitimately be deduced from the mere fact of sacrifice as attested in the Old Stone Age at least. In any case, the erection of buildings not designed nor adapted for the shelter or defence of their human builders was a radical innovation not derivable from the recorded habits of any beast or bird. Archæologically it is not traceable till neolithic times, and only rarely then.

The islanders of Malta, when still equipped only with stone tools, erected large and quite complicated edifices or enclosures of huge stones that may each weigh several tons. Lumps of stone hammered into the shape of balls that turn up round the sites had been used as rollers to transport the huge blocks, which are often beautifully dressed, and sometimes adorned with patterns like spirals or even scenic bas-reliefs; all of course with stone tools alone. Within the sanctuaries have been found stone vases and small stone statuettes of fat, recumbent persons that may be idols.

British societies, only a little better equipped than the neolithic Maltese—they had bronze weapons—expended almost as much labour on the construction of the famous sanctuaries of Avebury and Stonehenge, not to mention other less celebrated monuments, that rival in this respect the still earlier burial cairns mentioned on p. 91. Avebury is a level circular space, $14\frac{1}{2}$ acres in area, bounded by a ditch 30 feet wide, cut with only antler picks 20 to 30 feet into the solid chalk, with a bank 20 to 30 feet high outside it. The inner margin of the ditch was at one

time bordered by a ring of great stones enclosing
three smaller circles of still larger stone uprights—
one of these still rises 17 feet above the ground.   An
avenue of paired monoliths led up to the circles from
the river Kennet.

Stonehenge is smaller in area and less impressive
to behold, but must have cost no less social labour.
One of the component rings consists of substantial
monoliths of a peculiar blue stone that according to
all geologists must have been brought, and brought
by man, from the Presely Mountains in South-western
Wales.   Another ring is formed of local stones
indeed, but these have been neatly dressed with stone
mauls and attain a length of 28½ feet.   They support,
20 feet above the ground, stone lintels weighing up
to 6¾ tons.   These must of course have been dragged
into position up specially constructed ramps of earth,
the traces of which were disclosed by careful excavation.   The lintels were affixed to the uprights by
mortise and tenon joints carved in the stone in
imitation of contemporary woodwork.

Such stupendous monuments, obviously neither
domestic nor defensive, and infinitely more spacious
and permanent than any contemporary dwellings,
may safely be called sacred, though their precise use
be unknown.   But after this early outburst of temple-
building the barbarians of Europe have left us no
" sacred edifices " comparable in magnitude or
solidity with the stupendous fortresses of the Iron
Age.

In the Orient, temples can be traced back to 4000 B.C.
or thereabouts.

In Mesopotamia the centre of the barbarian village
that by successive reconstructions (p. 18) grew into
Tepe Gawra, " the Great Mound," near Mosul, was
occupied from its foundation, before 4000 B.C., by a
spacious building marked as a temple or a group of
shrines by its plan and the foundation for an altar.
At each reconstruction of the village the shrines were
rebuilt on a more lavish scale.   By about 3500 one

of three, grouped around a wide court and painted outside in different colours, measured externally 57 by 43 feet. The oldest cities in the Tigris–Euphrates delta grew up around similar temples that with the urban revolution in economy grew into veritable cathedrals. At Erech one, built just before 3000 B.C., already measured 245 feet by 100 feet over all, while a second, though only 73 by 57½ feet in area, stood on an artificial mountain of brickwork, or ziggurat, 35 feet high. These early temples were already decorated with reliefs in stucco and inlays in shell and imported wood, and furnished with altars for offerings and pediments for cult-images.

In the sequel a substantial proportion of the new wealth created by the new economy was devoted to enlarging and embellishing the temples of Mesopotamia. They remained the most sumptuous and imposing buildings in each city, even when they had to compete with the palaces of secular rulers. At Ur, for example, the artificial mountain had by 2000 B.C. become a tower of three stages, 62 feet high and measuring 205 by 141 feet at the base and at least 65 by 37½ feet at the top, where the high temple stood. The low temples were, of course, enlarged proportionately and enriched. Even when Ur had become a provincial city the king of Babylon after 600 B.C. rebuilt the ziggurat in kiln-fired brick and enlarged it. (But ere that, Sennacherib had built a palace at Nineveh measuring overall 650 by 630 feet.)

Of course a Mesopotamian temple was not only built as and with " offerings." The altar with channels for the blood leading therefrom shows even an illiterate archæologist that it was also the scene of periodical sacrifices of " fat-oxen " and also, as written texts make plain, of other sorts of food and beer. It was enriched with dedications of gold, silver, and precious stones and other kinds of valuables. Painfully few of these have been left for modern excavators to recover, but the literary sources show the temple functioning as a sort of bank. It was, of course, primarily the house of an imaginary deity. But the tablets dug up within it show that it served also as a school and library; written sources indicate that the staged tower was used as an observatory by astrologers, who, besides forecasting the future unsuccessfully, helped to regulate the calendar to the practical advantage of agriculture.

Temple foundations occupy a comparable place among the ruins of Bronze and Iron Age towns in other parts of Hither Asia. In Egypt the temples were at first overshadowed by royal tombs that were, of course, also temples of the divine kings. Only after 1500 B.C. do temples to the Sun and other deities begin to exceed in size and splendour the palaces as well as the tombs of Pharaohs, and their period of greatest magnificence coincides with the gradual decline of the national power and wealth after 1300 B.C. Their pre-eminence over secular buildings was lost when Alexander's Greek successors ascended the Pharaoh's throne.

But in Greece, while temples, as distinct from the palaces of " priest kings," were not built in the Bronze Age, during the Iron Age the largest and handsomest buildings in most cities were temples. Even before 600 B.C., when Crete was still just emerging from a Dark Age, a stone temple was built at Gortyna measuring 65 by 55 feet. And the great temple of Hera, in Samos, erected in 517 B.C., still without the aid of block and tackle (p. 40), covered a space of 366 by 177 feet. But the social estimation of Greek temples must be measured not so much by their size as by the patience and genius devoted to their embellishment. Even in ruins the temples of Athens, Pæstum, and Girgenti remain the most beautiful buildings in the Mediterranean world. And of course they were once enriched with the lavish offerings of pious votaries, though of their treasures only the poorest trifles—brooches, and such-like orna-

ments, and some rare bronze vessels and armaments—
have remained for the modern excavator to loot; the
gold and silver had been looted or otherwise converted
to secular use in antiquity.

Nevertheless, if temples in classical Greece consumed more of the social surplus than any other
class of building, the proportion of the whole thus
expended was probably substantially less than in the
Bronze Age of Egypt and Hither Asia. For a Greek
city enjoyed amenities—a water supply, theatre,
gymnasium (school), market place, town hall, baths—
not normally provided in an Oriental city. Even
private houses approach closer to the areas of
temples at Olynthus or Priene than at Lagash or
Erech.

In Roman times the balance shifted still further in
the same direction. Plenty of temples, shrines, and
altars were certainly set up to all sorts of gods in the
capital and throughout the Empire. Some were
larger and more ornate, but less beautiful, than their
Hellenic precursors. But for sheer magnitude, and
probably also for luxury of furniture, the Baths of
Caracalla and the Circus Maximus surpass any
Roman temple. It is even doubtful whether any
occupied as much space or cost as much as the
mansions of some millionaires, not to mention the
Emperors' palaces.

Neither Christianity nor Islam reduced the size and
number of ecclesiastical buildings, nor presumably
their social cost. Indeed, in Dark Age Europe the
cathedral resumed the central place in a city's topo-
graphy and economy that had been occupied by the
Sumerian temple in Bronze Age Mesopotamia. Hagia
Sophia in Constantinople and the Blue Mosque in
Baghdad are the most imposing monuments that survive of the early wealth of these capitals. But from
the mosques, altar and idols have alike been banished.
Even in a church, though the archæologist as such
cannot decide whether the images or pictures contained in them were worshipped, even he can see that

the altars are ill-adapted for the sacrifice of bulls. On the other hand, we do find libraries and schools attached to churches and mosques as well as buildings like hospitals designed to further the secular welfare of human beings. In other words, part of the wealth offered by the faithful was devoted to education or charity, instead of being consumed in burnt offerings and libations. This tendency has been accentuated with the further advance of civilization.

The Reformation discouraged extravagance in ecclesiastical architecture, and in many cases removed altars and images. Protestant churches in ruins will look, to future excavators, more like meeting-houses than physical abodes of a deity, though some will be found to ape traditional mediæval forms and furnishings. Though large churches, tabernacles, and synagogues are still being built, the biggest and handsomest remains in the ruins of a modern twentieth-century city will prove to have been universities, museums, art galleries, and concert-halls, not to mention the still more ornate picture-palaces and banks and the far vaster factories and arsenals. From the latest Russian cities no ecclesiastical remains will survive at all.

Five thousand years ago the major portion of the still very slender surplus available to society was devoted to the material housing and entertainment of gods or dead kings. Though the disposable surplus has multiplied many thousand fold in the succeeding millennia, the proportion expended on such substantial tenements and their furnishings would seem to have substantially declined. An archæologist might infer from this a decay of religion and worship. An historian, admitting literary evidence too, might reach a different conclusion: the object of worship would have been " spiritualized," and no longer conceived as desiring the flesh of bulls and the blood of rams and a habitation made with hands. Nor need he infer that the balance of the social surplus thus set free has been entirely expended in satisfying—even in a peculiarly elaborate and distinctively human way—impulses or appetites basically akin to those that seem to actuate the so-called lower members of the animal kingdom.

We might go on to describe portraits of the mammoth and woolly rhinoceros painted by contemporary artists in the gloomy recesses of French caves; female statuettes carved by Gravettians in mammoth-ivory and their descendants in pottery, stone, and plaster down to the present day; amulets, talismans, and beads of cowrie-shells, wolf's teeth, amber, lapis lazuli, gold, turquoise, pearls, or diamonds sought after from upper palæolithic times; earrings, nose-plugs, neck-rings, bangles, and anklets of ivory, shell, clay, bronze, gold, fayence, iron, and glass work at different times from the upper palæolithic; ochre, malachite, kohl, and other cosmetics, with the appropriate paint-tubes, vanity bags, and unguent flasks the use of which is even older; the wigs of the predynastic Egyptians and the first settlers in the Tigris–Euphrates delta and the razors used by the first citizens; beer-strainers, drinking-tubes, wine-jars, gin-bottles, and other receptacles for intoxicants that appear in the record from 3000 B.C.; tobacco pipes and teapots; harems provided in Egyptian tombs before 2500 B.C.; knuckle-bones, game-boards, dice; arenas, race-courses, and ball courts; flutes made by the Magdalenians and subsequently supplemented by drums, rattles, harps, trumpets, and horns; theatres and art galleries; compasses, balances, abaci, and retorts; museums and libraries, tablets, papyrus rolls and paper books; styli, pens, and printing-presses.

Most of these might be regarded as archæological indices of new wants or peculiarly human means of satisfying old needs. As an archæologist I am unable to decide how far the new wants are progressive, nor to detect any clear-cut lines along which the means of satisfying them have developed in 5,000 or 50,000 years. Did cowrie-shells add less to the charms or confidence of the Cro-Magnon than pearls to that of

the millionairess? Some authorities on art declare
that the reindeer-hunters' drawings have never been
equalled since. Others contend that the latest
American architecture (that was in any case anticipated in the first temple at Erech 5,000 years ago) is
really decadent and we must return to the Classical
models of Greece (that were apparently developed in
Egypt in the Pyramid Age). No one can decide
whether the predynastic Egyptian got more fun out
of his back-gammon than a contemporary derives
from two-up, nor whether the Hittites' chariot races
were less exciting or less popular than motor-cycle
events on a dirt track. Why should trousers now be
considered more becoming than loin-cloths, even in a
Mediterranean summer?

On the other hand, societies do seem to have discovered after several thousand years that flint-armed
darts accurately aimed with a spear-thrower secured
more meat than the most realistic picture of a
bison laboriously drawn in a dark cave. It apparently took longer to recognize that the dung of
oxen spread upon the fields ensured better crops
than the blood of oxen sacrificed on altars. But
in India and the Mediterranean basin people still
dedicate in temples and chapels female figurines
whose pedigree may plausibly be traced to the Gravettian statuettes of the last ice age! And you can buy
charms to-day that are doubtless just as efficacious as
the discs cut out of human skulls popular in neolithic
France!

Such ritual objects and their correlative rites express
the thoughts, or rather the emotions, of our helpless
palæolithic forerunners oppressed by the menacing
strangeness of an external world they still lacked the
equipment to control by more effectual means. Their
habitual use and repetition have preserved in fossil-
ized form mental states older perhaps than articulate
language or logical thinking itself, whatever specious
explanations theologians or patent-medicine vendors
may advance. Very reluctantly the most civilized

societies seem to be giving up the attempt to secure
material goods by spiritual means and spiritual ends
by material contrivances. The consequence may be
as beneficial to religion as to civilization, but that lies
beyond the vision of archæology.

CHAPTER VIII

RESULTS OF PROGRESS

THE progress that archæology can confidently detect is progress in material culture, in equipment. By its improvement human societies have with increasing success adapted themselves to their various environments and later adapted their environments to their own changing needs.

The effects of the advances set forth in the first five chapters are clearly cumulative; each new device and discovery has been a step to fresh and more efficient ones. But the process has not been continuous. The accumulation of buildings, one on the top of the other, in the settlement mounds of Hither Asia and Greece is at most sites interrupted by layers of debris and ashes that tell of the violent destruction of villages and cities by hostile men, by earthquake, or by flood. Throughout whole provinces the archæological record is interrupted by Dark Ages (cf. p. 10). At any given place or in any region archæology can and must recognize regression as well as progress in domestic architecture, rural economy, equipment, and means of communication. These phenomena doubtless represent natural or social cataclysms such as bulk so large in written history. But their effects are not cumulative. The regressions are generally only temporary. In a tell the layers indicative of destruction are subordinated to reconstruction. Or, at the worst, the archæologist can turn from the ruins of Mycenæan Greece to the flourishing Phœnician cities and Assyrian palaces, from the wasted towns of Roman Britain to Damascus and Baghdad. In archæological history evil appears as merely negative. Indeed, an archæologist might define evil as what is not cumulative. (A writer in *Nature* recently accused ordinary history of being

109

" instruction in the accumulated evil, violence, and intrigue of the ages.")

For us archæologists what accumulates is progressive. Now can we recognize any significant results, or rather concomitants of this material progress? During the long ages of the palæolithic stage Man seems to have become a better, at least a more human, animal. Our earliest recognizable forerunners in the lower palæolithic, Pekin men and Java men, were very ape-like creatures. A continuous barrel-shaped bar of bone projected vizier-like above the eyes, and from it the forehead sloped back to a very low vault. There is only room under this for a very small brain. The jowl, on the other hand, is enormous, and the great, chinless jaw is adapted for use as a bodily tool as well as for mastication. In Piltdown man these bestial features are less conspicuous; his brain-case differed little in capacity or external characters from that of modern man. But the great, chinless jaw found near the skull is even more ape-like than that of Pekin man. Finally, the Swanscombe skull, the latest human fossil attributable to the lower palæolithic, is regrettably incomplete. The hinder part is definitely more modern than ape-like, but forehead, face, and jaw, the most tell-tale parts, are missing.

In the middle palæolithic, Neandertal men, as represented in Europe and Upper Asia as far as Tashkent, have the same sort of bony vizier over the eyes and the same chinless jaw as Java and Pekin men. But the brain-case is much more capacious, the forehead less retreating, and the jaw, though chinless, less of a tool. By making flint tools men have been able to do without bodily tools, and the brain has grown with this use. The same sort of ape-like traits survive also in Solo man from Java, Rhodesian man (represented by a single skull found at Broken Hill), and the middle palæolithic inhabitants of Palestine. But some of the last-named exhibit more distinctively human attributes, such as an incipient chin.

From the very start of the upper palæolithic in Europe we find only modern men, quite like ourselves, and no more ape-like than we are.   In the succeeding 30,000 years no really significant bodily improvement is recognizable in human skeletons—and of course they are all that survive in the archæological record. We cannot even say that men have grown taller; for some Cro-Magnons stood 6 feet high.   On the other hand, it cannot be denied that we may have grown healthier.   The romantic conception of the naturally healthy savage has been exploded by prosaic ethnographers.   Anatomists have recognized traces of rheumatoid afflictions (arthritis), malformations (larkfoot), and dental decay on palæolithic skeletons. Similar disabilities have left their mark on bones from later periods more often than the layman would anticipate.   But there is not enough material to decide whether the incidence of, say, rheumatism was greater among British peasants in the neolithic stage than under the Roman Empire or to-day.   That the modern bourgeoisie are better off in this respect than the neolithic villagers of Orkney is of course obvious.

One point at least is clear: length of life has been increased, not by the magic of ochre nor megalithic burial rites, but by improvement in material equipment.   Prof. Vallois' table reproduced below illustrates this graphically for Europe.   It gives the percentage of persons dying within five age-groups at successive periods.

| | | *Age in years at death.* | | | | *No. of* |
Archæological period.	0–14.	14–20.	21–40.	41–60.	Over 60.	subjects.
Middle Palæolithic, % .	40	15	40	5	—	20
Upper Palæolithic, % .	24·5	9·8	53·9	11·8	—	102
Mesolithic, % . .	30·8	6·2	58·5	3	1·5	65
Early Bronze Age (Austria), % . .	7·9	17·2	39·9	28·6	7·3	273
Nineteenth Century (Lower Austria), % .	50·7	3·3	12·1	12·8	21	—
Twentieth Century (Austria), % . .	15·4	2·7	11·9	22·6	47·4	—

A similar increase in the individual's expectation of life could be illustrated from three successive phases of a barbarian Bronze Age at Hissar, in Iran.   Unfortunately no comparative figures have as yet been worked out for the Bronze Age citizens of Mesopotamia and Egypt for the Iron Age inhabitants of Greek and Roman cities, though plenty of material ought to be available.

That the human species has multiplied prodigiously as a result of material progress is perfectly plain. The regions habitable by lower palæolithic " man " must have supported even fewer and smaller groups than Australia; for the aboriginal inhabitants of that continent were far better equipped than any lower or middle palæolithic race or species. But their total numbers before 1800 are authoritatively estimated to have been only 200,000—a density of 0·03 per square mile. Favourably located upper palæolithic groups, like the Gravettians in South Russia and the Magdalenians in France and Spain, were doubtless substantially more numerous. In fact, from Europe five times as many measurable skeletons are available as from the middle palæolithic. By mesolithic times cemeteries attest relatively big communities: twenty-one interments, though only nine adults, were found at Teviec in Brittany and some sixty Natufians (who may have grown a little corn) were buried in the cave at Mount Carmel. Still, such cemeteries may cover a considerable time.

Small though they be, the enormous number of neolithic villages comprising eight to thirty-six households in itself indicates the brilliant success of the neolithic revolution in helping men to survive. Bronze by itself had no equally startling effect on societies that remained essentially barbarian in economy. The reaction of the urban revolution on population, on the contrary, may be inferred by comparing the mere sizes of the Bronze Age cities with those of neolithic villages as given on p. 55. The impression is confirmed by the cemeteries; in a single rustic cemetery in Egypt 500 graves, dated between 2560 and 2420 B.C., survived intact for modern excavators to examine! Then the influence of iron

tools upon the food supply among even barbarian
Europeans is again demonstrated by funerary evidence.
On the middle Rhine one cemetery alone is estimated
to have comprised 1,000 graves covering, on the most
generous chronology, only five centuries. But the
major increase in this period was again probably
urban. It is indicated sufficiently by the numbers
and growth of Phœnician, Greek, and Roman cities
mentioned on p. 50.

If in the sequel European cities were depopulated,
the loss was probably offset by the growth of Arabic
cities, to say nothing of India and China. The even
more dramatic growth of world population since the
eighteenth century is familiar, but a subject for a
book on statistics rather than archæology.

The most obvious consequence of technological
progress has been that the human species has grown
less completely dependent on inhuman nature, on the
external environment. A by-product, at least, of successful efforts at controlling natural processes by
technical means would seem to be a proportionate
diminution in attempts at controlling them by super-
natural means, if this phrase correctly describe the
tombs, temples, and ritual objects considered briefly
in Chapters VI and VII.

But if men have become less dependent on the
caprices of their physical environment, they have
grown more dependent on the social environment.
A savage stranded on a desert island would have had
a good chance of surviving; a civilized townsman in
like plight would soon perish of hunger and exposure
when his supply of matches, cartridges, and clothes
ran out. At the same time the social environment
has expanded with the improvement and acceleration
of means of communication and the development of
trade and intercourse sketched in Chapter V. Palæolithic hunters in the Crimea neither knew nor cared
how contemporary hunters fared in the Caucasus,
on the middle Don, or in the Balkans. The neolithic
villagers on Lake Neuchâtel were equally ignorant

and careless of the Danubians on the Upper Rhine, or their own distant kinsmen in Southern England, and perhaps even of closer relatives living along the Lake of Geneva. But an Egyptian carpenter or a Mesopotamian smith in the third millennium would suffer from disturbances in the lumber industry of Syria or the tin-mining in Eastern Iran. The tragic repercussions of the American financial crisis of 1931 and of two world wars are the logical outcome of the progressive operation of tendencies observable in the archæological record since the beginning of the Bronze Age at least.

Neither increased dependence on, nor the expansion of, society is altogether equivalent to a diminution of individual freedom. Even an archæologist can see that a Neandertaler was free to do very little. A palæolithic savage, if he were relatively free from social constraint (which an ethnographer would show cause to doubt), enjoyed very limited choice in the uses he could make of his freedom. There was at first no alternative to the constant struggle to snatch a bare livelihood, but each technical advance opened up new things to make and new ways of securing food. The Neandertaler could only hunt and collect; the upper palæolithic Magdalenian could theoretically hunt *or* fish; the neolithic Merimdian might choose to hunt or to fish or to farm. Finally specialization of crafts offered quite novel alternatives, as had the development of magical art perhaps in palæolithic times and the institutionalization of religion more certainly, but later.

Moreover, the elaboration of the toilet, the emergence of graphic arts, the multiplication of games, the luxuriance of religious ceremonies and funerary rites, finally writing and ciphering, offered mankind outlets for their superabundant energies, other than getting food and shelter and indulging in sexual intercourse, that were presumably alone available to lower palæolithic savages, as to their prehuman forerunners. These new activities to a greater or less degree must correspond to new interests, needs, and pleasures offering the individual fresh choices at any moment. The means for their satisfaction also became more diversified with cultural progress; for instance, in a barbarian cemetery the graves and their furniture all approximate to a single standard. But in the civilized cemetery of Olynthus we find both cremation and inhumation, half a dozen different types of grave, and an infinite diversity of grave-goods. In these directions, too, the barbarian is effectively freer to choose than the savage, the Iron Age than the Bronze Age citizen.

Again, it must be recalled that the growth in ability to make and do things that has been our central theme is a reflexion of the growth of knowledge of the world. The technical processes that archæology studies, from flint-knapping and bone-polishing to the construction of a cyclotron or the production of plastics, are each and all applications of Science, i.e., of a sort of systematized knowledge and experience of the outer world that works. The progressive perfection of the instruments of production expounded here is an expression and index of the cumulative growth of science that archæology can only infer. The diffusion of inventions, considered on pp. 57ff., is archæological proof of the pooling of human experience by which science grows. It shows that science always has been, as it is now, essentially international—the collective heritage of the human species as such, not confined to any breed or cultural group, but absorbing contributions from all.

The pursuit of scientific knowledge has now become avowedly a profession—a new alternative to hunting, farming, industry, trade, and war, and one that to some extent takes the place of the pursuit of sorts of " knowledge " that have been found not to work. Hence progress has presented the individual with a growing variety of possible things to do. In this sense progress may be said to have made human life richer and more diversified.

INDEX